T0220206

Android Studio New Media Fundamentals

Content Production of Digital Audio/Video, Illustration and 3D Animation

Wallace Jackson

Apress®

Android Studio New Media Fundamentals

Wallace Jackson
Lompoc, California, USA

ISBN-13 (pbk): 978-1-4842-1640-8   ISBN-13 (electronic): 978-1-4842-9867-1
DOI 10.1007/978-1-4842-9867-1

Library of Congress Control Number: 2015955164

Managing Director: Welmoed Spahr
Lead Editor: Steve Anglin
Technical Reviewer: Chad Darby
Editorial Board: Steve Anglin, Louise Corrigan, Jonathan Gennick, Robert Hutchinson,
    Michelle Lowman, James Markham, Susan McDermott, Matthew Moodie, Jeffrey Pepper,
    Douglas Pundick, Ben Renow-Clarke, Gwenan Spearing, Steve Weiss
Coordinating Editor: Mark Powers
Copy Editor: Jana Weinstein and Kim Burton-Weisman
Compositor: SPi Global
Indexer: SPi Global
Artist: SPi Global

Distributed to the book trade worldwide by Springer Science+Business Media New York, 233 Spring Street, 6th Floor, New York, NY 10013. Phone 1-800-SPRINGER, fax (201) 348-4505, e-mail orders-ny@springer-sbm.com, or visit www.springeronline.com. Apress Media, LLC is a California LLC and the sole member (owner) is Springer Science + Business Media Finance Inc (SSBM Finance Inc). SSBM Finance Inc is a **Delaware** corporation.

For information on translations, please e-mail rights@apress.com, or visit www.apress.com.

Apress and friends of ED books may be purchased in bulk for academic, corporate, or promotional use. eBook versions and licenses are also available for most titles. For more information, reference our Special Bulk Sales–eBook Licensing web page at www.apress.com/bulk-sales.

Any source code or other supplementary materials referenced by the author in this text are available to readers at www.apress.com. For detailed information about how to locate your book's source code, go to www.apress.com/source-code/. Readers can also access source code at SpringerLink in the Supplementary Material section for each chapter.

Printed on acid-free paper

Contents at a Glance

Contents

About the Author

Wallace Jackson has been writing for leading multimedia publications about his work in new media content development since the advent of *Multimedia Producer Magazine* nearly two decades ago, when he wrote about advanced computer processor architecture for an issue centerfold (a removable "mini-issue" insert) distributed at the SIGGRAPH trade show. Since then, Wallace has written for a number of other popular publications about his work in interactive 3D and new media advertising campaign design, including *3D Artist Magazine, Desktop Publishers Journal, CrossMedia Magazine, AV Video/Multimedia Producer Magazine, Digital Signage Magazine,* and *Kiosk Magazine.*

Jackson has authored a half-dozen Android book titles for Apress, including four titles in the popular *Pro Android* series. This particular Java 8 programming title focuses on the Java and JavaFX programming languages that are used with Android (and all other popular platforms as well) so that developers can "code once, deliver everywhere."

Jackson is currently the CEO of Mind Taffy Design, a new media content production and digital campaign design and development agency, located in North Santa Barbara County, halfway between clientele in Silicon Valley to the north and in Hollywood, "The OC," and San Diego to the south.

Mind Taffy Design has created open source technology–based (HTML5, JavaScript, Java 8, JavaFX 8, and Android 5) digital new media content deliverables for more than two decades (since 1991) for a significant number of leading branded manufacturers worldwide, including Sony, Tyco, Samsung, IBM, Dell, Epson, Nokia, TEAC, Sun, Micron, SGI, and Mitsubishi.

Jackson received his undergraduate degree in business economics from the University of California at Los Angeles (UCLA). He received his graduate degree in MIS Design and Implementation from the University of Southern California (USC). Jackson also received his post-graduate degree in marketing strategy at USC and completed the USC Graduate Entrepreneurship Program. The USC degrees were completed while at USC's night-time Marshall School of Business MBA Program, which allowed him to work full-time as a programmer while he completed his graduate and post-graduate business degrees.

About the Technical Reviewer

Chád(shod)Darby is an author, instructor, and speaker in the Java development world. As a recognized authority on Java applications and architectures, he has presented technical sessions at software development conferences worldwide (the United States, the United Kingdom, India, Russia, and Australia). In his 15 years as a professional software architect, he's had the opportunity to work for Blue Cross/Blue Shield, Merck, Boeing, Red Hat, and a handful of startup companies.

Chád is a contributing author to several Java books, including *Professional Java E-Commerce* (Wrox Press, 2001), *Beginning Java Networking* (Wrox Press, 2001), and *XML and Web Services Unleashed* (Sams Publishing, 2002). Chád has Java certifications from Sun Microsystems and IBM. He holds a BS in computer science from Carnegie Mellon University.

Visit Chád's blog at `www.luv2code.com` to view his free video tutorials on Java. You can also follow him on Twitter `@darbyluvs2code`.

CHAPTER 1

■ ■ ■

Enhancing Android Apps: Using New Media Assets

Welcome to *Android Studio New Media Fundamentals*. This book will take you through the foundation of new media principles and concepts so that you have a firm foundation regarding what Android Studio and the Android OS offer in the area of new media support. **New media**, sometimes referred to as **rich media** or **multimedia**, spans a number of professional artist occupations, which is why a multimedia producer has to be good at producing all forms of new media. This book seeks to enhance your knowledge of new media fundamentals and how they apply to Android Studio, so that you can make Android apps that are more stimulating to the senses—and thus more popular!

In this chapter, you'll take a look at the different forms of new media supported by the Android OS and how they can help your applications stand apart from the competition. You will also install professional-quality, open source software applications for each of the new media genres, so that you will be able to produce new media content for Android applications.

This book makes the assumption that you're already up to speed on Android Studio and its feature set—you have downloaded and installed it, and you are busy programming Android applications. I wrote this book to bolster your knowledge of the new media portion of the Android Studio equation, so that you will be able to add **custom multimedia assets** to your Android application instead of using the canned UI components that come with the operating system.

Throughout the rest of the book, there are two chapters per new media type (genre) to get you up to speed on the fundamentals and to learn how these new media types are supported in Android Studio; you'll also learn about the principles of data footprint optimization.

This book does not cover Android Studio, at least not directly; I assume that you have already downloaded and installed Android Studio, and that you know the basics. I have an *Android Apps for Absolute Beginners* (Apress, 2014) title that covers these topics if you need that foundational knowledge.

© Wallace Jackson 2015
W. Jackson, *Android Studio New Media Fundamentals*,
DOI 10.1007/978-1-4842-9867-1_1

New Media Genres: Multimedia Pie Slices

There are a number of different types (or genres) of new media, and all of these are supported in Java and JavaFX (which power Android, along with the Linux Kernel) as well as in Android OS. These support adding what I like to call new media "assets" to the Android application code. You're familiar with most of them I imagine: **digital images** like those on Pinterest or Instagram, or **digital audio** like that on Spotify or Pandora. **Digital video** can be used to stream movies or your favorite television show. Less prolific new media types include 2D vector or **digital illustration** media that looks like 2D cartoons, and 3D vector, or interactive 3D media, like you see people using on popular game consoles like Xbox to play sports or adventure games. All of these examples are high-sensory user experiences, so adding new media assets or elements to your Android application development process is how to take your app to the next level!

Separate Your App from the Crowd: New Media

The major advantage to incorporating new media assets into your Android application development in Android Studio is the visual and aural "wow factor" that you can add to an application. This sets it apart from other applications and generates a word-of-mouth marketing effort on the behalf of your users, and that you will not have to pay for. This is what I'd call a "windfall profit," and it is what this book targets to bring to your Android application development knowledge base and to your new media assets for Android Studio content production. For example, where digital imagery is concerned, instead of having a solid background color, use a subdued texture or a subtle color gradient, which is actually digital illustration, as you'll learn over the course (no pun intended) of this book.

Where digital audio is concerned, with custom audio user interface sounds for user interaction feedback, users will feel like they're more closely tied into, or are a part of, your Android application. Digital audio can enhance the user experience more than you are probably giving high-quality audio credit for!

Digital video and interactive 3D are more on the content production side of the application enhancement spectrum, rather than on the user interface design side of things; however, they are just as important. Digital video that is well optimized may play back more smoothly via slower connections, and interactive 3D, or i3D, applications are rare, other than popular 3D games.

Next let's take a look at the new media file formats the Android operating system includes. What I mean by "includes" is a decoder for the file format's codec (**code-decode**) is actually a part of the Android OS, and already installed on the hardware!

Android Studio New Media Support: File Formats

The key to bridging your new media content production to your Android Studio development environment is those new media file formats currently supported in Android 5 or later. Most of them are supported in Android 4. Many of these are also supported in earlier versions of Android, such as 1.6, 2.37, and 3.2. Devices running these versions of Android are becoming hard to find; soon all you will have to worry about is 32-bit Android 4.4 and

64-bit Android 5.4. Specialized versions of Android—such as the Android Wear, Android TV, or Android Auto SDK—support these same new media file (data) formats and codecs. So no worries there! Table 1-1 summarizes these popular new media file formats.

Table 1-1. *Android New Media File Format Support by Version*

New Media File Format	New Media Genre	Android OS Version Level
PNG8, PNG24, PNG32	Digital image	All OS versions
JPEG	Digital image	All OS versions
WebP	Digital image	Android OS 4.0+
GIF	Digital image	All OS versions
SVG	Digital illustration	All OS versions
OpenGL	3D	All OS versions
WebM (VP8, VP9)	Digital video	Android OS 2.3.3+
MPEG-4	Digital video & audio	All OS versions
MPEG-3	Digital audio	All OS versions
OGG Vorbis	Digital audio	All OS versions
FLAC	Digital audio	Android OS 3.1+
WAVE	Digital audio	All OS versions
AIFF	Digital audio	All OS versions
AMR	Digital audio	All OS versions

Android Studio digital image support currently includes JPEG, PNG, GIF, and WebP. You'll learn the attributes of each of these in Chapter 3, which covers digital imagery optimization, but I'm sure you know that JPEG is the most widely used digital image format, the CompuServe GIF is the oldest digital image format, and that PNG (Portable Network Graphics) is the newest digital image format. WebP is the same codec as your WebM video codec, except that it is compressing one frame, often called a "still" image.

Android Studio digital audio support currently includes MPEG4 Audio (M4A), MPEG3 Audio (MP3), Free Lossless Audio Codec (FLAC), OGG Vorbis, Windows Wave (WAV) Audio, Audio Interleaved File Format (AIFF) for Macintosh, and a number of others. You'll go over the attributes of each of these in Chapter 5, which covers digital audio data footprint optimization.

Android Studio digital video support currently includes MPEG4 AVC and WebM (VP8 and VP9). Whereas the digital audio support is expansive, the digital video support includes only two codec offerings—the same two that are supported in HTML5. Both codec offerings are open source, as Google purchased ON2 and made the VP8 and VP9 (WebM) codecs open source. MPEG patents expire in 2027 (all of them), although some have expired already. HTML5 and Android have licensed MPEG4, so you can use that in Android. You'll learn about each of these codecs in Chapter 7, which covers digital video data footprint optimization.

Android Studio uses Scalable Vector Graphics (SVG) for its digital illustration support; in fact, Java (via JavaFX) supports an entire library of classes that allow you to create, read, render, and animate SVG digital illustration data. You'll learn about the attributes of each of these in Chapter 9, when digital illustration data footprint optimization is covered.

3D modeling and animation support OpenGL, as well as all the 3D data formats that the OpenGL importers support, such as .FBX, .DAE (Collada), .3DS (3D Studio), .OBJ (WaveFront), .X3D, .STL (Stereolithography), and other open 3D geometry formats. You'll find out about each of these i3D data formats in Chapter 10, which covers 3D modeling, rendering, and animation concepts.

Downloading and Installing Your Software

I'm going to take a few pages in the second half of the chapter to show you a professional-level open source software package for each of the five new media genres that are covered in this book. This is so that if you do not have a software package that covers that type of new media development, you can download and install one that's free for commercial use and has all the professional features that a paid software package features. You will be amazed at the value that these software packages provide once you install and launch them.

Digital Image Editing and Compositing: GIMP

You need to have a digital imaging software package of one kind or another. If you do not own any digital imaging software, you can use the free-for-commercial-use GIMP 2.8.14, which is the current stable version, at least until GIMP 3.0 comes out some time in 2016.

To download GIMP 2.8.14, go to the **www.gimp.org** web site, and click the orange **Download** button; or alternately, click the **Downloads** link, seen on the right in Figure 1-1.

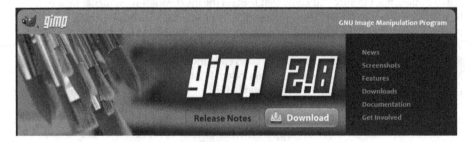

Figure 1-1. *Go to gimp.org and click the Download button*

Download the **GIMP-2.8.14.exe** installer file for your OS, and double-click it to start an installation. The installer can determine whether you need a 32-bit or a 64-bit version, so all you have to do is select a language that you want to use in the software, and then click the **OK** button. You'll get a **GIMP Setup** dialog, where you click the **Install** button to start the installation process.

If you want to customize the installation, you can click the **Customize** button and select exactly which components you want installed on your system. I recommend that you use a full install. This gives you a basic GIMP software installation with all the stable plug-ins, filters, and file export support.

Once the install process has completed, click the **Finish** button and create a shortcut icon for the Quick Launch taskbar for your OS, so that you can launch GIMP using a single click.

Digital Audio Editing and Effects: Audacity

You need to have a digital audio editing-and-effects software package for working with audio. If you do not own Reason, you can use the open source Audacity 2.1 software.

To download Audacity 2.1.1, which is the current, stable version, go to www.audacityteam.org and click the blue **Download Audacity 2.1.1** link, shown in Figure 1-2; or, alternately, click the **Download** tab under the Audacity logo.

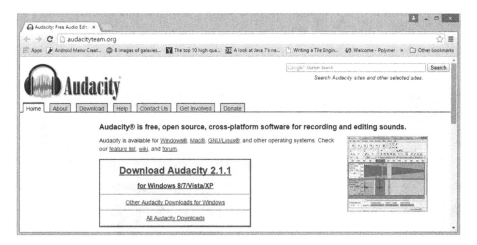

Figure 1-2. *Go to audacityteam.org and click Download*

Download the **audacity-win-2.1.1.exe** installer file (mine was for the Windows 8 OS). When it finishes downloading, double-click it to start the installation. The software is currently a 32-bit version, unless you are on 64-bit Linux, so all you have to do is select the **setup language** that you want to use in the software, and click the **OK** button. Next, you get the **Welcome to the Audacity Setup Wizard** dialog, which recommends that you close all of your open programs.

Click the **Next** button and review a licensing information screen, and then click the **Next** button to advance to a **Destination Location Specification** dialog, and then click **Next** to accept the default installation location in a `C:\Program Files(x86)\Audacity` folder. Click **Next** and the **Select Additional Tasks** dialog appears, allowing you to select options to **Create a desktop icon** and **Reset Preferences**.

Click **Next** to get the **Ready to Install** dialog, and then click the **Install** button to begin the installation process. The **Installing** dialog shows you the progress bar, and when your install is done, you get a dialog with an option to **Launch Audacity**. Select this option and click the **Finish** button. Take a look at Audacity—you will find that it is quite impressive.

Create a shortcut icon for the Quick Launch taskbar on your OS, so that you can launch Audacity using a single click.

Digital Video Editing and Effects: Lightworks

All Android developers should have a professional digital video editing and special effects software package of one type or another, whether it is Adobe AfterEffects, Sony Vegas Pro, or Apple Final Cut Pro. If you do not own any of these, you can download the free-for-commercial-use Editshare Lightworks 12.5.

To download Lightworks 12.5, go to **www.lwks.com**. If you do not have an account, create one so that you are able to download a free version of Lightworks 12.5. Click the blue **Downloads** button, seen at the top left of Figure 1-3, and then click the tab for the OS you're running.

Figure 1-3. *Go to lwks.com and click the Downloads tab*

In my case, this was Windows 8.1 OS. Click the version that matches your OS; for most of you, this should be **64-bit**.

To find out if your computer is 32-bit or 64-bit, right-click the **Computer** link in your Start menu (Window 7, XP, or Vista) and select **Properties**. In Windows 8.1 or 10, right-click the Windows menu icon, and select the **System** menu option, which displays a computer system information dialog.

On other operating systems, you can also look in the OS control panel under Computer or System for this information, which states whether the computer system is running a 32-bit or a 64-bit OS.

I clicked the 64-bit Download button to download the lightworks_12.5_full_64bit_ setup.exe installer file for Windows and double-clicked it to start the installation.

The first **Installer Language** dialog asks you to select a language that you want to use in the software. Click the **OK** button, which gives you the Welcome to the Lightworks Setup.

Click **Next**. In the **License Agreement** dialog, select an option that reads "I accept the terms of the License Agreement" and click the **Next** button again. Leave the default settings for the **Choose Components** dialog, and again click the **Next** button.

Leave the default settings for the **Choose Install Location** dialog, and then click **Next** to install Lightworks in a `C:\Program Files\Lightworks` folder. Click **Next**. A **Choose Start Menu Folder** dialog appears, allowing you to again accept an obvious Lightworks folder name default setting.

Once you click the **Next** button, you'll get a progress bar for an **Installing** dialog, where you can observe the installation process—if you're a speed reader, that is. Once the install is finished, click the **Next** button and then the **Finish** button.

Create a shortcut icon for your Quick Launch taskbar for the OS, so that you can launch Lightworks using a single click.

Digital Illustration and 2D Modeling: Inkscape

Since Java, JavaFX, and Android all 100% support SVG, you'll also need to have digital illustration software of one flavor or another, whether it is Adobe Illustrator, or Corel Draw, or Macromedia Freehand. If you do not own any of these, you can use the free-for-commercial-use Inkscape software package, which has all the features that you'll need to work on a professional level with SVG 2D vector data.

To download Inkscape 0.91, which is the current, stable version of Inkscape, go to **www.inkscape.org** and click the green **Download** button, seen in Figure 1-4; or alternately click the **Download** link at the top-left side of the web site. Inkscape supports 32-bit and 64-bit versions of its software; I assume you've ascertained the bit-level for your OS by now! The file I downloaded was the inkscape-0.91-x64.msi installer file. Double-click the installer file for your OS bit-level to begin.

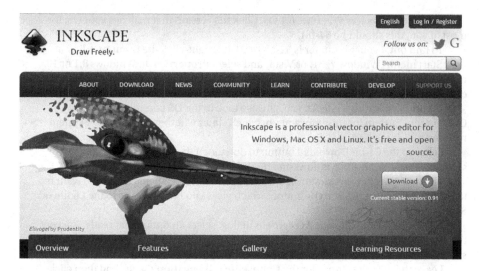

Figure 1-4. *Go to inkscape.org and click the Download button*

Once you launch the Inkscape installer, you get the **Welcome to the Inkscape Setup Wizard** dialog. Click the **Next** button to proceed to the **End-User License Agreement** dialog.

Select the "I accept the terms in the license agreement" checkbox, and click the **Next** button to proceed to the **Choose Setup Type** dialog. Click the **Typical** button and then the **Install** button to begin your installation. You see the **Installing Inkscape** dialog, which tells you what is being installed.

Once the install process has completed, click the **Finish** button, and create a shortcut icon for the Quick Launch taskbar for your OS so that you can launch Inkscape if you need it with just one mouse click.

3D Modeling, Rendering, and Animation: Blender

Java, JavaFX, and Android also support 3D new media via an open source 3D graphics library known as **OpenGL**. Therefore, you also need to have 3D modeling and animation software of one flavor or another, whether it is Autodesk 3D Studio Max, or Cinema 4D XL, or NewTek Lightwave. If you do not own any of these, you can use the free-for-commercial-use Blender software package, which has all the features that you need to work on a professional level with OpenGL 3D vector data and 3D formats.

To download Blender 2.76, the current stable version of Blender (prior to the next version 2.8, due out some time in 2016, and the predecessor to the much anticipated Blender 3.0), go to **www.blender.org** and click the blue **Download** button, or you can click the **Download** link, seen in Figure 1-5.

Figure 1-5. *Go to blender.org and click the download cloud*

Blender supports both 32-bit and 64-bit versions for the software; I assume you've ascertained the bit-level for your OS by now, so select the version that matches up with your OS. The file I downloaded was the blender-2.75a-windows64.msi installer file. Double-click the installer file to begin an installation.

Once you click the **OK** button, you'll get a **Welcome to the Blender Setup Wizard** dialog. Click the **Next** button, and proceed to the **End-User License Agreement** dialog.

Select the "I accept the terms in the license agreement" checkbox, and click the **Next** button to proceed to the **Custom Setup** dialog. Accept the default feature settings and click the **Next** button. Then click the **Install** button to begin installation. You see the **Installing Blender** dialog, which tells you what is being installed in real time.

Once the install process has completed, click the **Finish** button and create a shortcut icon for the Quick Launch taskbar for the OS, so that you can launch Blender 3D when you need it.

Summary

This chapter provided an overview of new media, both generally and in the context of Android Studio and the Android OS. You took a look at the different new media genres and discovered why they can help your Android apps stand out from the crowd. You looked at the different file formats that Android OS and Android Studio allow you to leverage to add visual and aural impact to your Android software creations.

In the second part of the chapter, you made sure that you had the leading, open source, new media content production software packages installed and ready to explore.

In the next chapter, you take a look at how pixels are stored in X,Y arrays and you learn about aspect ratios, color depth, anti-aliasing, and some of the other important imaging concepts.

CHAPTER 2

■ ■ ■

Digital Images: Concepts and Terminology

Now that you have an understanding of the primary areas of new media content and the file formats that Android Studio and the Android OS support, it is time to knock these pieces of the multimedia pie down one by one, two chapters at a time. Let's start with **digital imaging**, as it is the most prolific, popular, and mainstream type of new media. I'll cover everything in this chapter, from a pixel building block that makes up these raster images to the array that contains the pixels and the resolution and aspect ratio that defines that array. You will look at pixel characteristics such as location, color channel, alpha channel, color depth, and even advanced topics, like PorterDuff blending modes and NinePatchDrawables, both of which are supported in the Android API, with their own classes, methods, and constants.

You will learn the difference between 2D pixel-based raster images and a 2D (or 3D) vertex and line (or curve) –based vector image. Since you now own GIMP, I can show concepts in the book using GIMP, and you can follow right along with me.

Whereas a single pixel is just one point in space, which is called **1D**, or one dimensional (do not call your spouse this), an image is actually a **2D** array, or grid, of pixels, using both an X and a Y dimension.

Pixels: Your Digital Image Building Blocks

Digital images are made up of two-dimensional, or 2D, arrays (or grids) containing something called "pixels." This industry term **pixel** is the combination of two terms: **pictures** (commonly called "pix") and **elements** (shortened to "els"). Thus, the foundation for any digital image that you'll be working with in Android Studio is its picture elements. These pixels dictate everything about the digital image asset, like its file size, dimension, color, transparency, and shape. It is important to note that digital illustration assets aren't made up of pixels.

© Wallace Jackson 2015
W. Jackson, *Android Studio New Media Fundamentals*,
DOI 10.1007/978-1-4842-9867-1_2

Raster vs. Vector: Imagery vs. Illustration

Besides this term pixel, let's distinguish some key terminology related to pixels, right here up front, so that the difference between digital imagery and digital illustration are defined clearly. Images comprised of pixels are technically termed as **raster images**. The reason for this is because the array of pixels are "rasterized" by the device display screens that are displaying the pixels. These hardware devices include everything from an iTV set to a tablet to an e-book reader to a smartphone to a smartwatch to a Netbook to a laptop to a PC.

There is another type of digital image called a "vector" image, which is defined using mathematics rather than pixels. A vector image uses **points** in 2D space, which are called **vertices**, along with lines or curves that connect these vertices together to "draw" out your digital illustration, based on instructions, which are text-based and could be looked at as markup or code.

"Digital illustration" is what the **vector images** are popularly referred to in the new media industry. Vector imagery has its own "genre" of 2D software, called **digital illustration** software. You already downloaded and installed Inkscape in the previous chapter, so that you have it in place for Chapter 8. A 3D vector image is called a **3D rendering**, and an animated 3D vector project is called **3D animation**. Add programming logic and the 3D vector project is called **interactive 3D**, or **i3D**. You'll be taking a look at i3D new media in Chapter 10.

Rendering: Convert Vector Shape to Raster Image

Vector imagery can be converted into raster imagery by using a process called "rendering." A **rendered image** is inherently a raster image, and both 2D vector artwork, as well as 3D vector artwork, can be rendered into raster imagery, which as you know now, is pixel-based imagery. Raster imagery has a significantly larger data footprint than vector imagery, because instead of a concise set of text instructions (kilobytes), you have an array of pixels (megabytes) that you need to store to re-create your image.

At this point, all the concepts that are outlined in this chapter and the next can be applied, or do apply, to these pixel-format raster image assets.

When rendering vector artwork into a raster image format, it is important to remember to keep a backup of the "original" vector artwork, so that you can enhance or refine it more later on, and the re-render it again, at any time that you wish.

The primary advantage of vector illustration over raster imagery is that, since it's defined using math, it can scale up or down to any size. Scaling up, or "upsampling," 2D raster imagery causes what is termed **pixelation**. Next, let's look at arrays!

Resolution: The Number of Image Pixels

The number of pixels contained in your digital image assets should be expressed using a term called **resolution**. This is the number of pixels contained in your image. Images have a **width**, which is usually denoted using a **W**, or alternatively, by using an **X**, which stands for your **x-axis**, as well as a **height**, which is usually denoted using an **H**, or using a **Y** for the **y-axis**. The image resolution gives you the digital imagery's 2D dimensions.

The resolution of an image asset in Android Studio needs to be expressed by using two integer numbers, a Width, or an X, value, and a Height, or a Y value, in either XML markup or Java code. Image resolution is generally expressed using two integer numbers with an × in the middle. For instance, a VGA resolution is expressed by specifying **640×480**. Alternately, you could also use the word "by," such as **640 by 480** pixels.

Let's take a look at the basic mathematics of resolution so that you can see how to calculate the number of pixels there are in the image, which has a lot to do with the amount of memory it uses.

Doing the Math: Calculate Your Total Image Pixels

To find the total number of pixels that are contained in any 2D digital image, you will want to multiply width pixels by height pixels, or, in Java terms: `Resolution = Width * Height;` if you're writing code. Hopefully, you remember that **area of a rectangle** equation from grade school. Here it is again, in a professional Android digital imaging application context. When I was in grade school, I didn't realize that there were professional applications for what was being taught, so I didn't really listen, and therefore I had to go back and relearn my math and physics.

For an example, an HDTV-resolution 1920×1080 image contains 2,073,600 pixels if you multiplied the width and the height. If you're into digital photography, you'll be familiar with the term two **megapixels**, which is referring to 2.0 million pixels. This is essentially what HDTV resolution is giving you.

The more pixels that are contained in the digital image, the higher its resolution will be. Higher resolution images give the viewer more detail or image subject matter definition. This is why **HDTV** stands for **high-definition television**, and why the new 4K-resolution UHD TVs are **ultra-high definition**.

Next, let's take a closer look at some popular Android 5 consumer electronic device resolutions, which range from 240 to 4096 pixels, which is more than a seventeen-fold (i.e., 17 times) difference from a smartwatch device and a 4K iTV device. UI (user interface) design in Android needs to be able to "morph" between different resolutions. This is covered in my book *Pro Android UI* (Apress, 2014).

Matching Image Resolution to Android Devices

One objective in developing optimized digital image assets for use in Android Studio is matching the number of pixels in your digital image to the target hardware device that it is going to be viewed on. There used to be dozens of different resolution Android devices on the market. Recently, the number of different resolutions found on Android devices has been decreasing, which is great for developers. The reason for this is that more and more displays, especially smartphones, e-readers, and tablets, have been conforming to the three major iTV set resolutions. This has become possible since the display screen's pixel pitch (dot size) has been getting smaller, thanks to display technologies, such as OLED (organic light-emitting diodes). These flexible screens allow laser-printer-like resolution on display screens.

The first HDTV screen was what I call "pseudo HD," and was 1280×720 Blu-ray DVD resolution (1280×720 = 921,600 pixels, so you're talking almost 1.0 megapixels). For Android 5, a 1280×720 resolution is used in entry-level smartphones or in entry-level tablets, Netbooks, and laptops, so it's a common resolution. The reason for this commonality is because a lot of film, video, and TV content are being produced for this Blu-ray (1280×720) resolution. Matching content resolution to device resolution is going to give you the best image quality result, because there is zero pixel scaling. Pixel scaling is covered next.

The next HDTV resolution to appear in the market was the **True HD** resolution, which is a 1920×1080 resolution. As you know, this gives you 2.0 megapixels in contrast to the 1.0 megapixels that you get with 1280 pseudo HD resolution. Android OS devices that use True HD resolution include iTV sets, smartphones, mid-size tablets, and e-book readers. You also see this resolution on high-end Windows and Mac OS X laptops (or notebook computers).

The most recent type of high-definition display that has become available in today's marketplace is called the **Ultra HD**, or **UHD**, which is a 4096×2160 resolution. If you do the math, this display screen resolution contains 8,847,360 pixels. There will be UHD iTV sets out running Android TV SDK by the time you read this book, so interactive IMAX resolution apps are coming soon!

This is 9.0 megapixels in contrast to the 2.0 megapixels that you get with 1920×1080 True HD resolution. You already see Ultra HD resolution on UHD iTV sets, leading-edge smartphones, high-end tablets, and high-end e-book readers, and the latest UHD laptops (also called UHD notebook computers).

There's one other category of consumer electronic device called **smartwatches** that has resolutions of 320×320 and 400×400 (Huawei). Look for higher pixel density (pixel pitch) by 2016 in the smartwatch space, affording 480×480 pixel screens, and hopefully, 560×560 or 640×640 pixel screens by 2017.

Aspect Ratio: The 2D Ratio of W:H Pixels

Closely related to the number of pixels in your digital image is the **ratio of X to Y** in the digital image. This is called the **aspect ratio**. The concept of aspect ratio is more complicated than the image resolution, because it is the ratio of width to height, or **W:H**, within your image resolution dimensions. If you like to think in terms of an image x-axis and y-axis, it would be **X:Y**. Interestingly, Java, JavaFX, and Android use width and height, and X and Y, interchangeably (that is, inconsistently), so I can't make a recommendation as to how you should think about pixel referencing. This aspect ratio defines the shape of your image, and also applies to the shape of a display screen. For instance, a smartwatch has a square aspect (1:1), and a widescreen iTV set has a rectangular aspect (2:1).

A 1:1 aspect ratio digital image (or display screen) is perfectly square. Since this is the aspect ratio, by its very definition, a 1:1 aspect ratio is the same as a 2:2 or a 3:3 aspect ratio image. It is important to note that it is this ratio between these two numbers that defines the shape of the image or screen, not the numbers themselves, and that's why it is called an aspect ratio, although it's often called **aspect** for short. A 2:1 aspect ratio creates a **widescreen** aspect.

Screen Shapes: Common Display Aspect Ratios

Many HDTV resolution display screens discussed in the previous section use a 16:9 HDTV widescreen aspect ratio. However, some displays use a less wide, or taller, 16:10 (or 8:5, if you prefer the lowest common denominators) aspect ratio. Even wider screens will also surely appear on the market soon, so look for 16:8 (or 2:1, if you prefer a lowest common denominator) **ultra-widescreens**, which will feature a 2160×1080 screen resolution.

Early television screens were almost square; they used a 3:2 aspect ratio. Computer screens featured a 4:3 aspect ratio, such as Macintosh's 512×384 or the PC's 640×480 VGA screen resolution. Once you learn how to calculate aspect ratio in the next section of this chapter, you can check the math yourself.

As time goes on, PC displays keep getting wider. 2:1 widescreen 2160×1080 displays appeared in 2013 and it won't be long before UHD 2:1 displays (4096×2048) show up in the market. A recent aspect ratio change was introduced in 2015 with the Android smartwatch, which use 1:1 aspect ratio displays. Custom screen aspect ratios can get fairly extreme; you've all seen the 9:1 aspect ratio screens ringing the tops of sports stadiums.

Doing the Math: How to Arrive at the Aspect Ratio

An image aspect ratio is generally expressed using the smallest set or pair of numbers that can be achieved (reduced) on either side of the aspect ratio colon. If you paid attention in high school, when you were learning about the lowest (or least) common denominator, then the aspect ratio mathematics should be fairly easy for you to calculate.

I would do this mathematical matriculation by continuing to divide each side by two. Let's take a fairly weird 1280×1024 (termed **SXGA**) resolution as an example.

Half of 1280:1024 is 640:512; thus, half of 640:512 is 320:256. Half of that is 160:128, and half of that is 80:64. Half of that is 40:32, and half of that is 20:16. Half of that is 10:8, and half of that is 5:4. Therefore, an SXGA resolution uses a 5:4 aspect ratio.

Interestingly, all the preceding ratios are the same aspect ratio, and all are valid. Thus, if you want to take the really easy way out, replace that "×" in your image resolution with a colon, and you'll have an aspect ratio for the image. The industry standard involves distilling an aspect ratio down to its lowest format, as you've done here, as that is a far more useful ratio.

Color Theory: Using Pixel Color Channels

Within the image array of pixels that makes up your resolution and its aspect ratio, each of your pixels is holding color values using three **color channels** in Android, which uses an **RGB color space**. Color channels were originally used in digital image compositing programs like GIMP for compositing digital imagery for use on display screens, or to be printed using inks on printers, which use a different color space called **CMYK**. Color channels are sometimes referred to as "color plates" in the printing industry, due to older printing presses that used metal plates, some of which are still in use today. In GIMP, the color channels have their own channels palette, and allow you to work on just that color channel (or plate), which can be quite useful for special effects or other advanced image operations.

Android allows you to access the RGB components for each pixel using the drawables APIs, which I cover in my *Pro Android Graphics* (Apress, 2013) title. RGB stands for red, green, blue. Using the **additive color** model, these three colors of light can create any color in the visible color spectrum (think rainbow).

The opposite of additive color (RGB) is **subtractive color** (CMYK), which is used in printing and involves using inks. Inks subtract color from each other, rather than adding color, which is what happens when you combine colors by using light.

Using red and green as an example of additive color, results in **Red + Green = Yellow**. Using subtractive color, **Red + Green = Purple**. So as you can see, additive gives you brighter colors (adds light), whereas subtractive gives you darker colors (i.e., subtracts light).

To create millions of different color values using these RGB color channels, what you need to do for Android using Java code is to vary the levels or intensities for each of the individual RGB color values. I will show you how to do this for Android with hexadecimal notation after I cover the mathematics of RGB color, which gets into the bits and bytes of color.

The Mathematics of RGB Color: Multiplying Your Intensities

The amount, or numbers, of red, green, and blue values, or levels of intensity, of light that you have available to mix together determines the total number of colors that you are able to reproduce. For Android devices today, pixels can produce 256 levels of light intensity for each red, green, and blue (RGB) color. Color needs to be generated for each image pixel; thus, every pixel in an image has 256 levels of color intensity for each of these RGB (red, green, and blue) color data values.

Each of these RGB channels, plates, or planes, uses one byte, or eight bits, of color intensity data. Eight bits of data, as you know as an Android programmer, holds up to 256 different values, so you have 256 levels of brightness for each pixel's red, green, and blue color channel component.

The color intensity (brightness) data inside each of the digital image pixels is represented with a **brightness level** for each color. This can range between 0 (brightness turned off) and 255 (brightness fully on), and controls the amount of color contributed by each pixel for each of these red, green and blue colors in your digital image.

To calculate a total amount of available colors is easy, as it is again simple multiplication. If you multiply $256 \times 256 \times 256$, you get 16,777,216 colors. This represents unique color combinations of red, green, and blue, that you can obtain using these 256 levels (data values) per color that you have to work with across these three different additive color channels.

Representing RGB Color Values: Using Hexadecimal Data Values

In Android, you need to represent data for these 256 levels of brightness for each red, green, and blue pixel color channel. This is done by specifying 8 bits (worth) of numeric data value, which allows the Java code, or XML markup, to control color brightness variation for each of the red, green, and blue color channel values, from a minimum of 0 to a maximum of 255.

The number of bits that are used to represent a digital image pixel color can be coded by using **base 16**, or **hexadecimal**, notation. Base 16 counts from 0 to F, so that you have 16 values (bits) to represent color with. Two of these hexadecimal values give you 16 × 16 = 256 values, which is the number of levels of intensity that you have available for each RGB color channel.

In Android Studio, and conveniently, also in HTML5, CSS3, and JavaScript, this is done by using a hash or pound sign (#). For instance, to represent the color **BLACK**, which is all values off, or zero, in Java code or XML markup, this would look like the following:

```
colorValue = #000000 // Android, HTML5, JS, CSS3 Hexadecimal Color Value
```

The color **WHITE**, on the other hand, is all pixels fully on:

```
colorValue = #FFFFFF // Android, HTML5, JS, CSS3 Hexadecimal Color Value
```

The color **RED** turns on only the red channel pixels:

```
colorValue = #FF0000 // Android, HTML5, JS, CSS3 Hexadecimal Color Value
```

The color **GREEN** turns on your green channel pixels:

```
colorValue = #00FF00 // Android, HTML5, JS, CSS3 Hexadecimal Color Value
```

The color **BLUE** turns on your blue channel pixels:

```
colorValue = #0000FF // Android, HTML5, JS, CSS3 Hexadecimal Color Value
```

The color **Yellow** turns on red and green channels:

```
colorValue = #FFFF00 // Android, HTML5, JS, CSS3 Hexadecimal Color Value
```

In the next section of the chapter, you look at how these bit depths apply to different digital image file formats, such as an 8-bit GIF, or a 24-bit JPEG, or a 32-bit PNG. Android OS also supports 48-bit HDR (high-dynamic-range) color for cameras in some of the more advanced smartphone hardware coming out! As you may have surmised, 48-bit color uses 16-bit color channels.

Color Depth: Bit-Levels That Define Color

The amount of color available to each pixel in a digital image is referred to in the industry as the **color depth** of an image. Common color depths used in digital image assets include 8-bit, 16-bit, 24-bit, 32-bit, 48-bit, and 64-bit. Android supports three of these color depths: 8-bit using **GIF** and **PNG8**, 24-bit using **JPEG** and **PNG24**, and 32-bit using **PNG32**. The Android Camera 2 API also supports a new high-dynamic-range imaging (HRDI) format, which can hold 48 bits of color data. A 64-bit HDRI image supports three 16-bit (RGB) channels and a 16-bit alpha channel. Alpha channels are covered later in this section.

A high color depth image features the 24-bit color depth and thus contains 16,777,216 colors. File formats supporting 24-bit color depth include JPEG (or JPG), PNG, BMP, XCF, PSD, TGA, TIFF, and WebP. JavaFX supports three of these, JPG, PNG24 (24-bit), and PNG32 (32-bit). Using 24-bit color depth gives you the highest quality level. This is why I'm recommending the use of PNG24 or PNG32 for your Java games. Next, let's take a look at how you represent indexed image color using palettes!

Indexed Color: Using Palettes to Hold 256 Colors

The lowest color depth exists in 8-bit **indexed color** images. These feature a maximum of 256 color values, which is why they are 8-bit images, and use an indexed "palette" of colors, which is why they are called indexed color images. Popular image file formats for indexed color include GIF, PNG, TIFF, BMP, or Targa. The indexed color palette is created by the indexed color **codec** when you "export" your file from an imaging software package, such as GIMP. Codec stands for COde-DECode and is an algorithm that can optimize a file size to be smaller using **compression**.

Android OS supports two indexed color image formats: GIF and PNG. The way you convert 24-bit, true color image data to an indexed color image format (GIF or PNG) in Photoshop is to use the **File ➤ Save for Web** menu sequence. This opens your **Save for Web** dialog, which allows you to set a file format (GIF or PNG), the number of colors (from 2 up to 256), a color conversion algorithm (perceptual, selective, adaptive, or restrictive), the dithering algorithm (diffusion, pattern, or noise), and a number of other advanced options, such as progressive interlacing. I'd recommend using perceptual color conversion, 256 colors, and a diffusion dither algorithm for the best visual results.

To convert true color image data into indexed color image data using GIMP 2.8.14, use the **Image ➤ Mode ➤ Indexed** menu sequence. This calls up an **Indexed Color Conversion** dialog. This has fewer options than your Photoshop Save for Web dialog, but the important ones are there, so you can specify color depth and diffusion dithering. I recommend using the GIMP **Floyd-Steinberg** diffusion dithering algorithm. There is even an algorithm that reduces color bleeding, keeping image edges clean and sharp.

As an example of color depth, if you select 2 colors it would be a 1-bit (PNG1) image, 4 colors would be a PNG2 (2-bit color depth) image, 16 colors would be a 4-bit PNG4 color depth image, 64 colors would be a 6-bit PNG6, and 128 colors would be a 7-bit PNG7 image.

Next, let's take a look at the other major formats that are recommended for use in Android, 24-bit true color or 32-bit.

True Color: Using 24-Bit Color Imagery

One of the most widely used digital image file formats in the world is the JPEG file format, and it only comes in one flavor: 24-bit color. Other file formats that support 24 bits of color data include Windows BMP, TIFF, Targa (TGA), Photoshop (PSD), and PNG24. Since PNG also supports 8-bit (PNG8) or 32-bit (PNG32) color, I call a 24-bit PNG format PNG24, to be precise. Android supports two of these popular formats: JPEG and PNG.

Android true color (or truecolor) imagery uses an **RGB_888** color space (or color channels data configuration). The primary difference in these true color file formats supported in Android comes down to one, primary differentiating factor: lossy vs. lossless compression.

Lossy compression means that an algorithm, which is also called a codec, is throwing away some of the data to achieve a smaller data footprint. For this reason, save your original uncompressed file format using a lossless data format, prior to applying any lossy compression, in this case, JPEG.

Lossless compression—used by the PNG, BMP, TGA, and TIFF formats—doesn't throw away any original image data; it applies an algorithm that finds patterns that result in less data used, and that can 100% reconstruct all the original pixel values.

True color 24-bit images are used primarily with Android user interface design, or for actual applications content. They can also be used in other digital content that is displayed on Android devices, such as web sites, e-books, iTV programs, games, smartwatches, digital signage, and social media sharing forums.

Using more than one image in your Android application is called **image compositing**. Compositing involves using more than one image layer. The background or backplate image uses 24-bit image data. All the other layers in the compositing stack above a background plate needed to support transparency, and therefore, need 32 bits of data, which is also known as **ARGB** or **RGBA**.

This transparency is provided by a fourth channel, known as the "alpha channel." I'm going to introduce you to this in the next section of the chapter, as it's a key compositing concept.

If you are interested in learning more about using image compositing pipelines in Android, I cover this in detail in *Pro Android Graphics*. Using images for an Android application gives it a lot more pizzazz, but using an image compositing pipeline allows the next level of special effects and interactivity, to be achieved using digital imaging in your Android application development work process. This is a great reason for me to include coverage of alpha channels here!

True Color plus Alpha: Using 32-Bit Digital Images

Besides 8-bit, 16-bit, and 24-bit digital images, there are also 32-bit digital images. Formats that support 32-bit color data include PNG, TIFF, TARGA (TGA), bitmap (BMP), and Photoshop. I like to use PNG32 because it is supported in HTML5, Java, JavaFX, CSS3, JavaScript, and Android; whereas the other file formats are not integrated with the open source operating systems and browsers, like the PNG (pronounced "ping") format is. These 32 bits of image data include 24 bits of RGB color data, plus 8 bits of "alpha" or **transparency value** data, held in what is commonly referred to as an **alpha channel**.

Since you now know that 8 bits holds 256 values, it makes sense that an alpha channel holds 256 different levels of transparency data values for each pixel in a digital image. This is important for digital image compositing, because it allows layers that hold this 32-bit image data to allow some portion (from 0 to 255, or all of that pixel's color) of the color data to bleed through to (or to blend with) layers below.

Let's take a look at how four data channels translate in Android Studio. That's right, you're using hexadecimal notation, with two additional alpha slots, thus an **ARGB_8888** data format.

In Android Studio, as well as in HTML5, CSS3, JavaScript, and XML, hexadecimal for color plus alpha takes an ARGB format, so, the two alpha value positions need to go first.

For example, to represent the **TRANSPARENT** color, which is all values off, or 0 in code, it would look like this:

```
colorValue = #00000000  // Android, HTML5, JS, CSS3 Alpha+Color (ARGB)
```

The color **WHITE** with **50% translucency**, on the other hand, is all RGB pixels fully on for WHITE plus 8 (which is 7 when you count from 0) in each of the alpha channel data value slots:

```
colorValue = #77FFFFFF  // Android, HTML5, JS, CSS3 Alpha+Color Value
```

The color **RED** with **25% translucency** uses a value of 3 for each alpha channel slot, and turns on only the red channel pixels using FF, or fully on, and leaves green and blue fully off:

```
colorValue = #33FF0000  // Android, HTML5, JS, CSS3 Alpha+Color (ARGB)
```

The color **GREEN** and **37.5% translucency** use a value of 5 for each alpha channel, and turns on only the green channel pixels using FF, or fully on, and leaves red and blue fully off:

```
colorValue = #5500FF00  // Android, HTML5, JS, CSS3 Alpha+Color (ARGB)
```

The color **BLUE** with **75% translucency** uses a value of B for each alpha channel slot and turns on only the blue channel pixels using FF, or fully on, and leaves green and red fully off:

```
colorValue = #BB0000FF  // Android, HTML5, JS, CSS3 Alpha+Color (ARGB)
```

Next, let's take a close look at what alpha channels do.

Alpha Channels: Defining Transparency

Let's take a look at how alpha channels define digital image pixel transparency value, and how they can be used to composite digital imagery in Android. Alpha channels provide transparency inside of digital image compositing software packages such as GIMP, which I would term "static" use, but can also be used via PNG32 image assets to composite digital imagery in real time using open platforms such as Android Studio, HTML5, CSS3, Java, or JavaFX. I would term this "dynamic" use, as the code allows you to access the pixel transparency values in a millisecond, so you can animate the data in any way that you like; for example, in games, animated user interfaces, or interactive e-books.

Digital image compositing involves the seamless blending of more than one layer of digital imagery, and as you might imagine, per-pixel transparency is an important concept. Digital image compositing is used in graphic design, feature films, game design, and Android Studio application development.

Digital image compositing needs to be used when you want to create an image on your display that appears as though it is one single image (or an animation), but is actually the seamless collection of more than one composited image layer. One of the principle reasons you would want to set up image, or animation, composition is to allow you more control over various elements in an image composite by having components on different layers. Android Studio has a **LayerDrawable** class that provides exactly the same multilayer image compositing capability that you would find in GIMP, except optimized for use in your Android applications.

To accomplish multilayer compositing, you always need to have an alpha channel transparency value, which you can utilize to precisely control the blending of the pixel's color with the pixels in the same X,Y image location on other layers below it.

Like the RGB color channels, the alpha channel has 256 levels of transparency from 100% transparent (0) to 100% opaque (255). Each pixel has different alpha transparency data, just like each pixel has different RGB color data.

Almost everything in Android Studio that can be drawn on a display screen supports alpha channel values via an ARGB_8888 digital image format using hexadecimal notation. This includes user interface elements, themes, styles, and drawables. I showed you how this is formatted using the hash (pound) sign, and you can use this hexadecimal numeric format in both your XML markup and in your Java code. Remember this, because few developers use it!

PorterDuff: Algorithmic Blending Modes

There is another powerful aspect of image compositing called a **blending mode**. Any of you who are Photoshop or GIMP users have seen that each layer in a digital image compositing software package is able to be set to use a different blending mode. Blending modes are algorithms that specify how the pixels for a layer are blended (mathematically) with the previous layers (underneath that layer). The Android API has a **PorterDuff** class that allows you to access all of these blending mode algorithms in your Android applications.

These pixel blending algorithms take into account a pixel transparency level; so, between the two image compositing controls, you can achieve virtually any compositing result that you want in Android Studio.

The major difference with Android is that blending modes can be controlled interactively, using custom Java programming logic. This is the exciting part for Android developers.

These powerful PorterDuff class blending modes include XOR, SCREEN, OVERLAY, DARKEN, LIGHTEN, MULTIPLY, and ADD. *Pro Android Graphics* covers how to implement PorterDuff blending modes inside a complex image compositing pipeline, if you are interested in diving into this area of Android in greater detail.

Smoothing Edges: Anti-Aliasing

Anti-aliasing is an imaging technique that is also implemented by using an algorithm. What the algorithm does is find where two adjacent colors meet along an edge, and blend those pixels around that jagged edge. Anti-aliasing adds **averaged colors** along the edge between two colored areas to visually smooth those two colors together along that (formerly) jagged edge. This makes the jagged edge appear to be smooth, especially when the image is zoomed out and the pixels aren't individually visible. What anti-aliasing does is trick your eyes into seeing smoother edges, to eliminate what is commonly called "the jaggies." Anti-aliasing provides impressive results, using few (usually fewer than eight) intermediary averaged color values for those pixels that lie along edges within the image and need to look smoother.

By "averaged colors" I mean colors or a spectrum of color that is between the two colors, intersecting along the edge that is being anti-aliased. I created a visual example of anti-aliasing for you to show the resulting effect.

I first created the seemingly smooth red circle, seen in Figure 2-1, against a yellow background. I zoomed into the edge of that circle, and then I grabbed this screenshot.

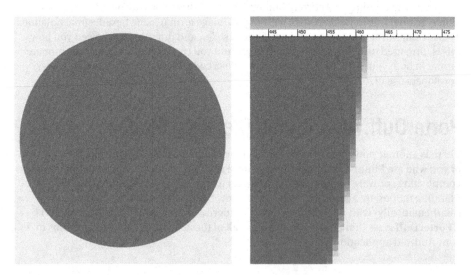

Figure 2-1. A zoomed in view (right) shows anti-aliasing effect

I placed this alongside of the zoomed out circle to show the anti-aliasing (orange) pixel values, for colors between red and yellow, the color values bordering each other along an edge of the circle. Notice that there are seven or eight averaged colors used to create this visual effect.

One of the tricks that I utilize in Android to implement my own anti-aliasing effect is to use the **Gaussian Blur** via the **ConvolutionMatrix** class in Android. This also works in GIMP and Photoshop. Be sure to use a low blur value (0.125 to 0.375) on the object (as well as its alpha channel) with jagged edges.

This provides the same anti-aliasing that you see in Figure 2-1, and not only that, it "blurs" the alpha channel transparency values as well.

Blurring the alpha channel allows that alpha channel to anti-alias a 32-bit image object with any background imagery you may be attempting to seamlessly composite it against. Next, let's look at image optimization!

In the next chapter, you dive into how to use alpha channel data in Photoshop and GIMP; it just gets more exciting.

NinePatch Assets: 9-patch Digital Images

There is another type of digital image "drawable" in Android OS called the **NinePatchDrawable**; it allows Android developers to develop a special type of morphable PNG8, PNG24, or PNG32 image asset. An image asset created with the Android **Draw 9-patch tool** is essentially an XY-axis-independently-scalable PNG raster image that uses nine distinct quadrants within the image asset to support axis-independent scaling.

Due to a built-in NinePatchDrawable class, and **NinePatch** class support, Android can automatically resize the developer's 9-patch image assets to accommodate the contents of any Android View object, inside of which the developer has placed a 9-patch image asset as a background (or source) image asset reference.

This is accomplished via algorithms that exist inside of the Android NinePatch class and the Android NinePatchDrawable class, as well as inside of the Draw 9-patch software tool. This tool can be found in the /sdk/tools subfolder in the Android SDK folder.

An example of a use for a NinePatch image asset is on the inside of a background image using an **android:background** XML parameter, which is commonly used with the standard Android Button widget. Button UI widgets almost always need to stretch, in at least one dimension and often in both X and Y dimensions, in order to accommodate text using different character strings and different font styles and sizes.

This NinePatchDrawable object uses Android's recommended PNG digital image format; it also includes an extra one-pixel-wide border to hold the scaling guidelines. To be recognized by Android as 9-patch image assets, they need to be saved using the **.9.png** file name extension. The one-pixel border that I mentioned is not visible to your end users, and instead is utilized by the Android NinePatch class algorithm to define the areas of the image asset that are **scalable**, and the areas of the image asset that are **static** (fixed, that is, not scalable).

NinePatch Class: Creating NinePatch in Android

The Android NinePatch class is a direct subclass of the Java java.lang.Object base class, which means that it was coded uniquely to define NinePatch objects in Android. An object constructed using the Android NinePatch class allows Android to scale and then render a 9-patch image asset using nine discreet scalable sections or areas within the 9-patch PNG image asset. As you might have guessed, this class is stored inside of the **android.graphics** package. Its class hierarchy looks like this:

```
java.lang.Object
  > android.graphics.NinePatch
```

A great analogy is a compass. The four corners for these 9-patch images (at NE, NW, SE, and SW) are unscaled; whereas the four edges (N, E, S, or W) are scaled along one axis. The middle of the compass (the 9-patch image) is scaled along both of its axes, just like any normal image is scaled in Android OS.

Optimally, the middle of your 9-patch source image asset is 100% transparent. This is so that a 9-patch can provide a scalable image framework around an open, compositable content area for your View object, in case you are using that View as a miniature compositing container, since some View objects, like an **ImageView**, can have a source and a background image (as well as other elements) that would show through transparent areas.

The Android Draw 9-patch tool gives developers a simple, useful tool for creating NinePatch images using a WYSIWYG (What You See Is What You Get) image editor. Let's look at this now.

Draw 9-patch: Create a NinePatchDrawable Image

This section covers how to create a 9-patch image asset using the Android Draw 9-patch tool. You need a source PNG image with which to create a NinePatchDrawable object; I provide a sample PNG32 image asset named **NinePatchFrame.png**. If you are interested in creating 9-patch image assets, I will take you through it in the final section of the chapter so that you understand the basic 9-patch tool work process.

Start by locating your Draw 9-patch tool in the Android SDK folder hierarchy in the **tools** subfolder. Once you open the tools subfolder, you see the **draw9patch.bat** Windows batch file, which is what you need to launch to run draw9patch.

There are two ways to open your PNG32 images for 9-patch development. You can drag your PNG image into your Draw 9-patch window and onto the drop-it arrow in the center, or you can use the **File ➤ Open 9-patch** work process to locate the file in your NinePatch images subfolder.

Once you find the **NinePatchFrame** source image PNG asset, select it and click the **Open** button. You see your Draw 9-patch software, with the PNG file in the editor and preview area. The left pane is where you edit, creating **patches** using one-pixel black lines, defining patches, or scaling areas, as well as your center content area, defined by padding lines.

The right pane is the resulting 9-patch preview area, as shown in Figure 2-2, where you can view what your 9-patch image asset will look like after it is scaled. To define a patch, click in the transparent top border, and then drag toward your left to draw a black line that defines the X-dimension scalable patch. Once you draw an approximation of what you want, you can fine-tune it using the fine lines at each end of the line segment.

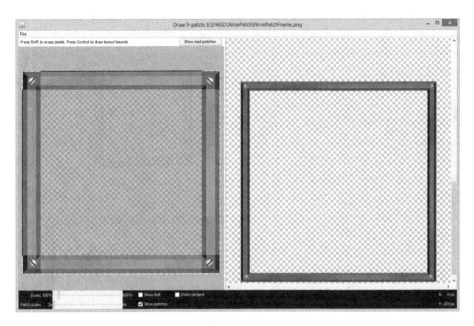

Figure 2-2. *Defining patches in the Android Draw 9-patch tool*

Place your cursor over the fine line and it changes into a double arrow. Click and drag a grayed-out area until it fits pixel-perfectly with the transparent area in the center of the **NinePatchFrame.png** image. You can also right-click to erase the previously drawn line.

Look for a check box next to the **Show patches** option; select it to turn this feature on. As shown in Figure 2-2, this provides colors in your selected areas using a combination of purple and green. This makes it clear which area in your image asset is being affected. You can see that several other useful controls exist at the bottom of the editing pane. These include a **Zoom** slider, which allows you to adjust the zoom level of the source graphic in the editing area, and a **Patch scale** slider, which allows you to adjust the scale for your preview imagery.

The **Show lock** option allows you to visualize the non-drawable area of the graphic when you mouse-over it. The **Show content** option highlights your content area in a preview image, where purple shows the area that content can be placed.

Finally, at the top of the editing area, there is a **Show bad patches** button. This adds a red border around patch areas that may produce artifacts in the image when it scales. Visual excellence for your scaled images can be achieved if you strive to eliminate all of these bad patches in your 9-patch design.

Figure 2-2 shows a 9-patch image asset with the top and the left one-pixel border black-line definitions. As you can see, due to the **Show patches** option, I have now defined the static areas, and scalable areas with surgical precision.

Also notice in Figure 2-3, in the right-hand side preview, that the result of the 9-patch image definition is giving me a professional scaling result. I grabbed the scrollbar on the right side of my screen and pulled it down, so you can see the 9-patch scales in both portrait and landscape shapes.

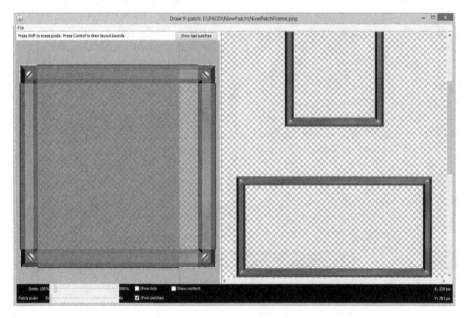

Figure 2-3. *Draw 9-patch preview shows axis-independent scaling*

You can also see the padding areas that I have defined, using the one-pixel black border lines on the right and the bottom of the editing pane. Figure 2-3 shows that I'm in the process of drawing a one-pixel black border line segment on the bottom side to define an X dimension for the center padding area for a 9-patch image.

Summary

In the second chapter, you took a look at digital image concepts, terms, and Android classes that implement image assets. You looked at pixels, resolution, aspect ratio, color channels, color depth, alpha channels, anti-aliasing, blending modes and PorterDuff, and NinePatchDrawable objects. In the next chapter, you'll take a closer look at image **data footprint optimization**.

CHAPTER 3

■ ■ ■

Digital Image Assets: Data Footprint Optimization

Now that you have an understanding of the fundamental concepts, terms, and principles of digital image new media content and the file formats that Android Studio and Android OS support, it is time to get a bit more advanced and take a look at **data footprint optimization**. Data footprint optimization involves saving your digital image asset in a way that it takes up the least amount of data storage; that is, it has the smallest possible file size. In this chapter, you will be looking at data footprint optimization for all the new media areas, because the smaller you make the new media assets for your Android application, the smaller that Android application will be in the Google Play Store, and the faster it will download, load into memory, and run once it is in memory.

You will look at the difference between 2D pixel-based raster images and a 2D (or 3D) vertex and line (or curve)-based vector image. Since you now own GIMP, I can show concepts in the book using GIMP—and you can follow right along with me.

Optimizing Digital Imagery: Key Factors

There are a number of technical factors that affect **digital image compression**, which is the process of using a codec or algorithm that looks at your image data and finds a way to save it as a file that uses less data. A codec **encoder** essentially finds "data patterns" in an image and turns these patterns into a form of data that the **decoder** part of the codec can algorithmically reconstruct original image data from. A great codec is part of the data footprint equation, but image data that you hand a codec to compress can make the difference!

Let's start out by discussing image attributes that affect a data footprint the most, and examine how each of these aspects can contribute to the data footprint optimization for any given digital image. Interestingly, these are similar to the order of digital imaging concepts that you covered during Chapter 2.

© Wallace Jackson 2015
W. Jackson, *Android Studio New Media Fundamentals*,
DOI 10.1007/978-1-4842-9867-1_3

Image Resolution: Number of Pixels in the Array

The most critical contributor to the resulting image file size, or data footprint, is the number of pixels, or the **resolution**, of your digital image. This is logical because each of these pixels needs to be stored, along with the color values for each of the RGB color channels. Thus, the smaller you can make your image resolution, while still having good detail, the smaller the resulting file size will be, because there is less data to be compressed, as an image is simply an array of pixel values.

As you know, a raw uncompressed image size is calculated using the formula width × height × color channels. There are three RGB color channels for 24-bit RGB images and there are four ARGB color channels for 32-bit imagery. It is important to note this raw (uncompressed) image data footprint also happens to be the amount of **system memory** that your image will occupy once a decoder decompresses its compressed format into system memory.

The key to data footprint optimization at this level is to follow my advice in Chapter 2, and match image resolution to the device that the image is targeted to be viewed on.

What virtually everyone out there is doing wrong is using print resolution imagery, which uses camera resolution CCDs (charge-coupled devices), to create digital image file data, which contains 24 to 48 megapixels. Popular HD display devices, as you have already learned, have a 1- or 2-megapixel resolution, or, in the case of 4K or UHDTV, 9-megapixel resolution at the most. For this reason, you should downsample print resolution to a 4K resolution, at the most, using bicubic (Photoshop), or cubic (GIMP) interpolation algorithms.

With new **super-fine dot-pitch** displays on most of today's Android devices, you are even able to **upsample** (upscale) an HDTV (2-megapixel) image up to UHD (8 megapixels) and there will still be enough pixels present for your resulting image to look quite crisp and photorealistic on any fine dot-pitch display.

The most optimal way to downsample an image is by what's termed "power of two," which is like binary: 2, 4, 8, 16, and so on. So if your camera gives you a 8192×6144 (48-megapixel) image, downsampled by 2 on each axis to 4096×3072, or by 4 on each axis to 2048×1536, or by 8 on each axis to 1024×768.

A lot of people ask me why a lot of smartphones use a 2560×1440 resolution. The answer is that manufacturers know that most video content is in Blu-ray (1280×720) format, and if you double that on each axis, you get 2560×1440, so a full-screen video is scaling by a power of two and gets the best image quality because there are no partial pixels involved in the scaling algorithm. Mathematically, this means that there is only even division, no remainders if you will, so edges remain crisp and clear. This holds true for upsamples or downsamples.

Image Color Depth: Color Channels for Each Pixel

Since each of the pixels in an array (resolution) for an image in Android has a color depth of either 8 bits (one channel of color data), 24 bits (three channels of color data), or 32 bits (four channels of color and alpha data). Therefore, this is the next most important contributor to an image data footprint. I suspect this is one of the reasons indexed color (8-bit or one color channel) images are still widely used, usually in the PNG8 image format, which features a superior, lossless compression algorithm, at least when compared to the GIF codec.

As you know, lossless compression algorithms such as PNG lose zero image data and maintain 100% quality; whereas a lossy compression algorithm, such as JPEG and WebP, throws away data, and therefore image quality, to achieve more data compression.

PNG32: Using True Color Images that Have an Alpha Channel

If you are using **compositing layer** image assets—that is, PNG32 images that include an alpha channel containing an object mask or that contain translucency (variation) special effects—there is only one option in Android, which is the PNG32 image format. These images have the most data to compress, so hopefully the PNG codec will do a good job at compressing the image data.

Each image contains a unique collection of pixel values, so you never know if any given image is going to compress well or not, because it is ultimately all math in the algorithm.

In general, the more chaos (fine details) the image has, and the more clearly defined edges the image has, the larger the resulting file size will be. The fewer sharp pixel transitions (edges), and the more smooth color gradients it contains, as smooth transitions are easier to compress, the smaller your resulting file size will be.

True Color Images: Using 24-Bit Color Depth with JPEG and PNG

The same considerations as to chaos and edges goes for 24-bit images, but there is another codec besides PNG if you want to get smaller file sizes, albeit by throwing away original image data and introducing visual artifacts. As you know, the JPEG is a lossy codec, but it can give you smaller file sizes at the cost of visual quality. So, if you are seeking the highest quality digital image results, try to utilize the PNG codec and format, as it does not introduce artifacts (unless you use PNG8 and diffusion dithering, which are looked at in more depth later on in the chapter when you delve into indexed color images). As I mentioned, some PNG24 images compress quite well; you really just need to run the data through a codec and find out!

So if you are using 24-bit images, with no alpha channel data, and the range of color used in the image is limited, then consider using a PNG8 indexed color format, with 256 colors and diffusion dithering, to reduce the data footprint by 300% to 400% with no quality loss. Indexed color imagery looks great on super-fine dot-pitch displays, as the dithering dots are too small to see!

This same super-fine dot-pitch advantage also applies to JPEG compression artifacts, making them too small to see. It is important to note, however, that Android recommends using PNG24 or PNG32 over JPEG whenever possible, to make application image quality the best that it can possibly be, which is what Android wants as the end objective, as it is in a fierce competition as far as operating systems are concerned. Android OS has been steadily winning new market share since it was released; let's keep it that way!

Indexed Color: Using Up to 8-Bit Color with Diffusion Dithering

Indexed color images can simulate true color images, if the total number of colors that are used to make up the image do not vary too widely. As you know, indexed color imagery uses only 8 bits of data, or 256 colors, to define the image pixel color plate. This is done using a **palette** of optimally selected colors. For instance, if you have a picture of clouds in a sky, or a beautiful sprawling forest, or a bouquet of roses, there may be enough slots in the palette to reproduce these few colors and the gradients they contain, especially if you use diffusion dithering and have a device with a super-fine dot-pitch.

Depending on the number of colors that are used in a 24-bit source image, using 256 colors to represent an image containing 24-bit color depth could cause an effect called **banding**. This is where the transfer between adjoining colors in your resulting palette is not visually gradual, and thus doesn't appear to be a smooth color gradient.

Indexed color images have the option to visually correct for banding, which is called **dithering**. As you know already, dithering is an algorithmic process for creating dot patterns along the edge between any adjoining colors within the image. This tricks your eye into thinking that there is a third color being used.

Dithering gives you the maximum perceptual number of colors using the 256 color palette. If each of those 256 colors borders on each of the other 256 colors, you could simulate the maximum number of 65,536 colors (16-bit color), but this seldom occurs. You can still see the potential for creating additional colors, and you will be amazed at the results that the indexed color codec and data formats (PNG8 or GIF) can achieve in compression scenarios involving certain imagery, featuring the right number of colors and subject matter that is optimal for indexed color.

Let's optimize a true color image, such as the one that's shown in Figure 3-1, and save it using the **PNG5** indexed color image format, to show you diffusion dithering. You will take a look at the dithering effect on the driver's side rear fender on the Audi 3D image, as it contains a gray gradient.

Figure 3-1. *A PNG24 image created with Autodesk 3DS MAX to compress as PNG5*

It is interesting to note that it is permissible to use less than the 256 maximum colors that can be used in an 8-bit indexed color image. This is often done to further reduce your digital image data footprint.

For instance, an image that can attain great results by using only 32 colors would actually be a 5-bit image, and would technically be called a PNG5, even though this format itself is generally called PNG8, for its maximum 256-color usage level.

You will set this indexed color PNG image, which is shown in Figure 3-2, to use 5-bit color (32 colors, or PNG5). This is so you can see the dithering effect clearly. As you can see in an image preview area on the left side of Figure 3-2, dithering creates dot patterns between your adjacent colors in order to create additional colors. In this case, it's grayscale value.

Figure 3-2. *Select Diffusion Dither and 32 colors creating PNG5*

Also, notice that you can set a **percentage of dithering**. I often select either the 0% or 100% setting; however, you can fine-tune the diffusion dithering effect anywhere between these two extreme values.

You can also choose between dithering algorithms; as you probably have surmised already, the dithering effect is created using dithering algorithms that are a part of the indexed file format (PNG8 in this case) encoder's compression routines.

I prefer diffusion dithering, which has a smooth effect, especially along irregularly shaped gradients, as can be seen in the Audi's driver's side rear fender shown in Figure 3-2.

You can use a **Noise** option, which is more randomized, or a **Pattern** option, which is less randomized. A **Diffusion** option usually gives the best results, which is why I use it when I'm using indexed color (which is not that often, as I use PNG32).

Dithering, as you might imagine, adds data patterns into an image, which are more difficult to compress. This is because smooth areas in an image, such as gradients, are easier for the compression algorithm to compress than sharp transition (edges) areas, or random pixel patterns, such as dithering, or "noise" from your digital camera's CCDs, for instance.

Therefore, applying the diffusion dithering option will always increase the data footprint by a few percentage points. Be sure to check the resulting file size with and without dithering applied (selected in the Export dialog), to see if it is worth the improved visual result that it affords. Notice there's also a **Transparency** option (check box) for indexed color PNG imagery. It is important to note that the alpha channel that is used for PNG8 images is 1-bit (on or off), and not 8-bit, as with PNG32.

Image Alpha Channel: Pixel Transparency Channel

The final concept you've learned about so far that can increase data footprint in an image is adding an alpha channel to define transparency for compositing. This is because adding an alpha channel adds an 8-bit transparency channel to your image. If you need an alpha channel to hold transparency for an image, there's not much choice but to include this alpha channel data.

If your alpha channel contains all zeroes or uses an all-black fill color (which will define your alpha channel as being completely transparent), or contains FF values, or uses a white fill color (which would define your alpha channel as completely opaque), you would essentially (in practical use) be defining an alpha channel that does not contain useful alpha data values.

The transparency alpha channel therefore needs to be removed, and an opaque image needs to be defined as a PNG24 digital image rather than as a PNG32, saving one data channel.

Finally, alpha channels that are used to mask objects in the RGB color channels of your digital image compress very well. This is because these alpha channels are largely areas of white (opaque) and black (transparent), with some gray values, along the edges between the two colors to anti-alias the mask.

These gray areas, which contain your anti-aliasing values in the alpha channel, provide a visually smooth edge transition between the object in the color channels of your image with any background color or background imagery that is used behind it.

The reason for this is because the alpha channel image's mask contains an 8-bit **transparency gradient** ranging from white to black. This defines levels of transparency, which should be thought of as per-pixel blending (opacity) strength.

Therefore, these medium-gray values on the edges of each object in your mask, which is contained in this alpha channel, will essentially average the colors of the object edge and any target background. It can do this no matter what color or image data value each pixel might contain.

This provides real-time antialiasing with any target background that might be used, including animated backgrounds, since this alpha channel–based transparency blending would get calculated on every animation frame by a CPU capable of doing millions (if not billions) of operations each second.

Now that you've gone over concepts, formats, APIs, terms, and data footprint optimization for digital images, you are ready get into digital audio—another popular new media genre—next.

Summary

In this chapter, you took a look at digital image data footprint optimization concepts, principles, and Android formats that compress and decompress your digital image assets. You looked at how your resolution, color channels, color depth, and alpha channel can contribute to your data footprint reduction.

In Chapter 4 you will learn about **digital audio new media** concepts, terms, and principles, so that you can add digital audio assets to your Android Studio applications.

▓ ▓ ▓

Digital Audio: Concepts and Terminology

Now that you have an understanding of the fundamental concepts, terms, and principles of digital image new media content and the file formats Android Studio and the Android OS support, it is time to get into digital audio new media content, and the many file formats that Android Studio and the Android OS support. You will look at the concepts behind both analog audio and how it is digitized into digital audio, as many of these analog and digital waveform concepts apply across both audio mediums.

You will look at how waves, or air, create audio and analog audio concepts, such as amplitude and frequency, and at digital audio concepts, such as samples and resolution. You will look at advanced digital audio concepts such as bit-rate, streaming, HD audio, and captive digital audio. Finally, you'll look at all the powerful digital audio formats supported by Android 5 OS, which you can use to develop Android Studio new media applications.

Audio Concepts and Terminology

In this chapter, I am going to get you up to speed on both analog audio concepts and terminology, as well as digital audio concepts and terminology. You will see how the transition is made between analog and digital audio using a process called sampling, which those of you who do sound design and music synthesis are already quite familiar with. You will look at encoding audio using bit-rates, streaming, and the new 24-bit HD Audio standard now being used for broadcast radio and satellite. You will also learn about the audio codecs (audio file formats) supported in Android Studio. You will go over digital audio data footprint optimization in Chapter 5. I need to make sure that you have a deep understanding of the digital audio new media assets that you will eventually be creating, optimizing, and "rendering" using Android's digital audio compatible classes, such as **SoundPool** and **MediaPlayer**.

Foundation of Analog Audio: Sound Waves of Air

Just like digital imaging, digital audio can be quite complex, especially at the professional level. Part of this complexity comes from the need to bridge analog audio technology and digital audio technology together, because modern-day devices are digital.

© Wallace Jackson 2015
W. Jackson, *Android Studio New Media Fundamentals*,
DOI 10.1007/978-1-4842-9867-1_4

Analog audio used to be generated by using speaker cones of different sizes manufactured using resilient membranes made out of one space-age material or another. These speakers would generate **sound waves** by vibrating, or pulsing, them into existence. Our ears receive this analog audio, still used at live concerts, in exactly the opposite fashion: by catching and receiving those pulses of air, or vibrations, with different wave lengths, and then turning them back into "data" that our brain can process. This is how you "hear" these sound waves, and our brain then interprets these different audio sound wave **frequencies** as different **notes** or **tones**.

A sound wave generates a different tone depending on the **frequency** of that sound wave. Wide, long, or infrequent wave cycles produce lower (bass) tones; whereas a more frequent (shorter) wavelength produces a higher (treble) tone. It is interesting to note that different frequencies of light produce different colors, so there is a very close correlation between analog sound (audio) and analog light (colors), which also carry through to digital production techniques and principles.

The volume of the sound wave is predicated upon the **amplitude** of that sound wave, or the **height** (vertical size) of the wave. Thus, frequency of sound waves equates to how closely together the waves are spaced, along an x axis, if you look at it in 2D, and the amplitude equates to how tall the waves are, as measured along the y axis.

Sound waves can be uniquely shaped, which allows them to mimic different sound effects. Your baseline sound wave type is called a **sine wave**, which you learned about in high school math with the sine, cosine, and tangent math functions.

Those of you who are familiar with synthesizer keyboards are aware that there are other shapes of sound waves that are used in sound design, such as the **saw wave** that looks like the edge of a saw (hence its name), or the **pulse wave**, which is shaped using right angles, resulting in immediate on and off sounds that translate into pulses.

Even randomized waveforms, such as **noise**, can be used in sound design to obtain an edgy sound result. As you might have ascertained using data footprint optimization knowledge from Chapter 3, the more "chaos" or noise that is present in your sound waves, the harder they are to compress for the codec. This results in a larger digital audio data footprint for that particular sound.

Next, you're going to take a closer look at how an analog sound wave is turned into digital audio data by using sampling, which is one of the core tools of sound design and music synthesis.

Digital Audio: Samples, Resolution, and Frequency

The process of turning analog audio (sound waves) into digital audio data is called **sampling**. If you work in the music industry, you have probably heard about a type of keyboard (or rack-mount equipment) called a "sampler." Sampling is the process of slicing an audio wave into segments, so that you can store the shape of that wave as digital audio data by using a digital audio format. This turns an infinitely accurate sound wave into a discreet amount of digital data; that is, into zeroes and ones. The more zeroes and ones used, the more accurate the reproduction of the infinitely accurate (original) analog sound wave. The sample accuracy or resolution determines the number of zeroes and ones used to reproduce the analog sound wave (you will get to that topic next).

Each digital slice of the sampled sound wave is called a **sample**, because it takes a sample of a sound wave at that exact point in time. The precision of the sample is determined by the amount of data that is used to define each wave slice's height. Just like with digital imaging, this precision is termed your resolution, or more accurately (no pun intended), the **sample resolution**.

Audio sample resolution is defined as 8-bit, 12-bit, 16-bit, 24-bit, or 32-bit. In digital imaging and digital video, the resolution is quantified by the number of color channels; and in digital audio, the resolution is quantified by the bits of data that are used to define each of the audio samples being taken. In digital images, more colors yield better quality; and in audio, a higher sample resolution yields better sound reproduction.

Thus, higher sampling resolutions, or using more data to reproduce a given sound wave sample, yields a higher audio playback quality at the expense of a larger data footprint.

This is the reason why 16-bit audio, termed "CD quality audio," sounds better than 8-bit audio; just like true-color images always look better than an indexed color image.

In digital audio, there is now a 24-bit audio sampling, known as "HD audio," in the consumer electronics industry. HD digital audio broadcast radio uses a 24-bit sample resolution, so each audio sample, or slice of a sound wave, contains a 16,777,216 potential sample resolution. Some the newer Android devices now support HD audio, such as the smartphones that you see advertised featuring "HD quality" digital audio playback.

In order for an Android hardware device to play back this HD audio format, you must have 24-bit audio hardware; so I recommend using 16-bit audio, as you will see in Chapter 5 when you look at audio data footprint optimization.

Besides a digital audio sample resolution, you also have a digital audio **sampling frequency**. This defines the number of samples, at any given sample resolution, that are taken during one second of sample time. In digital images, sampling frequency is analogous to the number of pixels that are contained in an image. Sampling frequency can also be called the **sampling rate. CD quality audio** is defined as using a 16-bit sample resolution and a 44.1 kHz sampling rate. This is taking 44,100 samples, each of which contains 16 bits of sample resolution, or the potential maximum 65,536 data values, for digital audio data held in each sample.

Let's do some math to find out the number of bits of data in one second of raw (uncompressed) digital audio data. This can be calculated by multiplying the 65,536 sample resolution by the 44,100 sample frequency. This yields a data value of 2,890,137,600 values, which are available to represent one second of CD quality audio. Audio codecs compress this down to an amazingly small file size, as you will see in Chapter 5.

The point is that the exact same trade-off that you have in digital imaging exists using digital audio. If you include more data, you get a higher-quality result, at the cost of a larger data footprint. Fortunately, audio codecs do a better job, giving an even better quality-to–file size result than digital imaging codecs provide.

Common audio sample rates for the digital audio industry include 8 kHz, 11.25 kHz, 22.5 kHz, 32 kHz, 44.1 kHz, 48 kHz, 96 KHz, 192 kHz, and recently, 384 kHz. As you may have guessed, I like to use the ones that are evenly divisible by the power of two (8-bit), and so I gravitate toward 8 kHz (low quality), 32 kHz (medium quality), and 48 kHz (high quality), as you'll see in Chapter 5.

Lower sampling rates, such as 8 kHz, 11 kHz, or 22 kHz are optimal for sampling "voice-based" digital audio, such as a movie dialog track or an e-book narration track, for instance.

Higher audio sample rates, such as 32 kHz or 48 kHz, are more appropriate for music and possibly sound effects, such as rumbling thunder, which absolutely needs high-dynamic range for high-fidelity reproduction.

Some sound effects can get away with using a lower 11 kHz or 22 kHz sampling rate, as long as the sampling resolution used is 16-bit quality. Ultimately, you'll have to use your ears as your guide during the digital audio optimization process to ascertain your aural quality to digital audio asset file size trade-off.

Digital Audio Data: Transmission and Digitization

As I mentioned, an industry baseline for superior audio quality is known as CD quality audio, which is defined as a 16-bit data sample resolution and a 44.1 kHz data sample frequency. This is what was used to produce audio CD products way back in the 20th century, and it is still used as the minimum quality standard today. There's also the more recent HD audio standard using a 24-bit data sample at a 48 kHz or 96 kHz sample frequency. This is used today in HD radio, as well as in HD audio–compatible Android devices such as "Hi-Fi" HD audio smartphones. Since the Android OS supports 16-bit 48 kHz audio, I tend to use this as my high-quality audio compromise, because the data footprint is smaller. Let's take a look at how to use these assets in Android Studio. Do you store the audio inside the app or stream it from a remote server? What audio playback or streaming bit-rate would you use?

Digital Audio Transmission: Streaming Audio or Captive Audio?

Just like with digital video, which covered in Chapters 6 and 7, digital audio assets can either be **captive**, or contained within the Android application APK file, with audio files in a /raw folder, or digital audio assets can be **streamed** by using remote data servers. Similar to digital video, the upside to streaming digital audio data is that it can reduce the data footprint of the Android application APK file. The downside is reliability. As you will see in this book, many of the same concepts apply equally well to images, audio, and video.

Streaming audio saves data footprint, because you do not have to include all that data-heavy new media digital audio in your APK file. Thus, if you are planning on coding a Jukebox application, you would want to consider streaming digital audio data, as you would not want to pack your song library into your APK file because it would be 10 gigabytes (for a large library).

Otherwise, for application audio, such as user interface feedback sounds, gameplay audio, and so forth, try to optimize your digital audio data so that you can include it inside of your APK file as a captive asset. In this way, it is available to your application users when needed. You'll learn about optimization in Chapter 5 after audio fundamentals in this chapter.

The downside to streaming digital audio is that if your user's connection (or your audio server) goes down, your audio file might not be present for your end users to play and listen to! This reliability and availability of a digital audio data stream is a key factor to consider on the other side of this streaming audio vs. captive digital audio decision.

The same trade-off is discussed in Chapter 7 for digital video data footprint optimization considerations.

Streaming Digital Audio Data: Optimally Setting Your Bit-Rates

One of the primary concepts in streaming your digital audio is the bit-rate of the digital audio data. Again, this is very similar to digital video; the reason you are learning about digital audio before digital video is because digital video is made up of both digital image sequences and digital audio, so I need to cover those concepts and terminologies first.

The digital audio bit-rate is defined during compression by the settings that you give to a codec during an optimization work process. You'll look at data footprint optimization, as it relates to digital audio, in Chapter 5, where you'll use Audacity 2.1 to optimize your own sample digital audio assets.

As with digital video, digital audio files that need to support a lower bit-rate to accommodate slower bandwidth networks are going to have more compression applied to the digital audio data, which results in a lower audio quality level.

These play back smoothly across a greater number of devices. This is because if there are fewer bytes for transfer, over any given data network, then there are also fewer bytes to be processed by the CPU in the hardware device as well.

As a processor gets faster, it can process more bytes per second. As a data bandwidth connection gets faster, it can more comfortably send or receive more bytes per second.

Therefore, it is important to remember that you are not only optimizing your file size for fast network transfers, but you are also optimizing the new media asset for an amount of system memory that asset will use, as well as the amount of processing cycles the CPU will use to process the new media asset's data (play audio, play video, display image, render vectors, etc.).

Digital Audio in Android: File Formats

There are considerably more digital audio codecs in Android than there are digital imaging codecs (there are only four image codecs: PNG, JPEG, GIF, and WebP). Android audio support includes .MP3 (MPEG-3) files; .WAV (PCM or Pulse Code Modulated) Wave files; .MP4 or .M4A (MPEG-4) files; .OGG (OGG Vorbis) audio files; .MKS (Matroska) files; .FLAC (Free Lossless Audio Codec) files; and .MID, .MXMF, and .XMF MIDI (Musical Instrument Data Interface) files, which technically aren't really even digital audio data at all.

Let me explain what MIDI is first. It is not a format that you will likely use in your Android Studio application, but it underlies the history of digital audio and is unique in its digital player piano performance playback approach. I'm including it in this chapter because it has some unique and highly data footprint–optimized applications. After that I'll cover all of the sampled digital audio formats.

MIDI: Musical Instrument Data Interface

MIDI stands for Musical Instrument Data Interface and it is one of the very first ways that you could work with audio using your computer. The origins of MIDI date all the way back to the 1980s, so MIDI has been around for several decades now.

The first computer to feature MIDI dataport hardware was the Atari ST 1040. This computer allowed me to plug my keyboard synthesizer (at the time it was a Korg M1) into its MIDI port. MIDI allowed me to play and record performance data using the computer, which used MIDI data format along with audio software known as a MIDI **sequencer**, because it sequenced playback data.

MIDI files contain no sample data; that is, they contain no audio data, only the **performance data**. When this performance data is played back into the synthesizer by the computer, using the MIDI hardware (interface, cables, and ports) the synthesizer generates the audio tones using the MIDI performance data.

MIDI records when and which keys on the synth or sampler keyboard are pressed, along with the keypress duration, how hard it is pressed (aftertouch), and similar performance nuances.

When MIDI files are played back through the synthesizer, it replicates the exact performance of a performer or composer; even though that person is no longer playing the performance track, the computer is. You can play your instrument track, record your instrument play performance using MIDI data, and the MIDI sequencer will then play the performance for you, while at the same time, you play a second instrument track alongside of the first one.

MIDI enables songwriters to assemble complex musical arrangements using only their computers. This is certainly less expensive than hiring a studio and musicians. If you want to be a songwriter, you can download open source MIDI software called **Rosegarden** at http://rosegardenmusic.com. Not only is Rosegarden a MIDI sequencer, but it also includes **music notation**, also known as **scoring**. This means that you don't have to know how to write notes and clefs on staffs in order to publish your music!

The Android OS supports **playback** of MIDI files, but does not implement a MIDI class for their creation. Hopefully, this will change in the future, but as it sits right now, it would not be an easy job to code MIDI sequencers in Android Studio; however, some people on the coding forums are talking about it.

For that reason, MIDI is beyond the scope of this book. I cover it here only to educate you on the history and scope of digital audio support in Android Studio (Android OS). MIDI holds an important role in the evolution of digital audio and it is a key component of **music synthesis** and **sound design**.

MPEG-3 Audio: The Popular MP3 Data Format

The most popular digital audio format in Android Studio is the **MP3** digital audio file format. Most of you are familiar with MP3 digital audio files that are found on music download web sites, like Napster. Most of us have collected songs in this format to use on popular MP3 players and in our CD-ROM music collections.

The reason that this MP3 digital audio file format is popular is because it has a relatively good **compression-to-quality ratio** and because the codec needed to play MP3 audio files is found everywhere, even in the Android OS.

MP3 would be an acceptable format to use in your Android Studio application as long as you get the highest quality level possible out of it by using the optimal encoding work process on audio data footprint optimization using the open source Audacity 2.1 audio software (covered in Chapter 5). Because of software patents, Audacity can't include MP3 encoding software or distribute MP3 software from its own web site, so be sure to download and install a free **LAME encoder** for Audacity.

It's important to note that the MP3 codec outputs a **lossy** audio file format (like JPEG does for images), where some of the audio data, and thus quality, is discarded during the compression process and cannot be recovered.

Android does support an open source **lossless** audio codec called **FLAC**. This stands for **Free Lossless Audio Codec**. Support for FLAC is as widespread as MP3 due to the free nature of the software decoder (codec is encoder-decoder, as in **CO**de-**DEC**ode).

FLAC: The 24-Bit Free Lossless Audio Codec

FLAC uses a fast algorithm, so the decoder is highly optimized for speed. FLAC supports 24-bit audio, and there are no patent concerns for using it. This is a great audio codec to use in Android Studio if you need high-quality audio with a reasonable data footprint. FLAC supports a range of sample resolutions, from 4-bit data per sample, up to 32-bit data sampling. It also supports a wide range of sampling frequencies, from 1Hz to 65,535 Hz (or 65 kHz), using 1 Hz increments, so it is extremely flexible. From an audio playback hardware standpoint, I suggest using a 16-bit sample resolution, and either a 44.1 kHz or a 48 kHz sample frequency, unless you are targeting HD audio.

FLAC is supported in Android 3.1 or later. Therefore, if your end users are using current Android devices, you should be able to safely utilize this FLAC codec. It is possible to use completely lossless new media assets in Android application development (such as PNG8, PNG24, PNG32, or FLAC), as long as your application is targeting Android 3.1 or later hardware devices. Next, let's take a look at another impressive open source codec.

OGG Vorbis: A Lossy Open Source Audio Codec

Another open source digital audio codec supported by Android is the **OGG Vorbis** format. This lossy audio codec is brought to you by the Xiph.Org Foundation. The Vorbis codec data is most often held inside an **.OGG** audio data file extension, and thus, Vorbis is commonly called the Ogg Vorbis digital audio data format.

Ogg Vorbis supports sampling rates from 8 kHz to 192 kHz and supports 255 discrete channels of digital audio. As you now know, this represents 8-bits worth of audio channels. OGG Vorbis is supported across all Android versions or API level releases.

Vorbis is quickly approaching the quality of MPEG HE-AAC and Windows Media Audio Professional and it is superior in quality to MP3, AAC-LC, and WMA. It's a lossy format, so the FLAC codec has superior reproduction quality over Ogg Vorbis, as FLAC contains all the original digital audio sample data.

MPEG-4 Audio: Advanced Audio Coding (AAC)

Android supports all MPEG-4 AAC (Advanced Audio Coding) codecs, including the **AAC-LC, HE-AAC**, and **AAC-ELD**. These should each be contained using an MPEG-4 file container (.3gp, .mp4, or .m4a file extensions). AAC-LC and HE-AAC can be decoded with all versions of Android. The AAC-ELD is only supported after Android OS 4.1. ELD stands for **Enhanced Low Delay**; this codec is intended for use in real-time, two-way communications applications, such as a digital walkie-talkie or a Dick Tracy–style smartwatch app.

The simplest AAC codec is AAC-LC (**Low Complexity**) codec, which is the most widely used. This is sufficient for most digital audio encoding applications. AAC-LC yields a higher quality result, at a lower data footprint, than the MP3 codec.

The most complicated AAC codec, HE-AAC (**High Efficiency**) codec supports sampling rates from 8 kHz to 48 kHz, and both **stereo** and **Dolby 5.1** channel encoding. Android decodes both V1 and V2 levels of HE-AAC. Android can also **encode** audio using the HE-AAC-V1 codec in Android devices later than version 4.1.

Because of software patents, Audacity does not include an MPEG-4 encoder. Be sure to download and install the free **FFMPEG 2.2.2 encoder** for Audacity from http://lame.buanzo.org before you start Chapter 5, where you'll be using the latest Audacity 2.1.1!

MPEG-4 AMR: Adaptive Multi-Rate Audio Codecs

For encoding speech, which usually features a different type of sound wave than music does, there are also two other **AMR** (**Adaptive Multi-Rate**) audio codecs, which are extremely efficient for encoding things like speech or "short-burst" sound effects.

There is an **AMR-WB** (Adaptive Multi-Rate Wide-Band) codec in Android that supports nine discrete settings, from 6.6 kbps bit-rates up to 23.85 kbps, sampled at 16 kHz. This is a pretty high sampling rate where voice is concerned! This is the codec to use on narrator tracks if you're creating interactive e-book Android Studio applications, for instance.

There's also an **AMR-NB** (Adaptive Multi-Rate Narrow-Band) codec in Android that supports eight discrete settings, from 4.75 kbps to 12.2 kbps audio bit-rates sampled at 8 kHz, which is an adequate sample rate if the data going into the codec is of high-quality or if resulting audio samples do not require a high quality due to the noisy nature of the content (e.g., a bomb blast).

PCM Audio: Pulse-Code Modulation Codec

Finally, Android supports PCM (pulse-code modulation) codecs, commonly known as Windows WAVE (.WAV) audio format or Apple AIFF (Audio Interchange File Format). Most of you are familiar with this lossless digital audio format from one of these two popular operating systems. It is lossless because there is *zero* compression applied. PCM audio is commonly used for CD-ROM content, as well as telephony applications. This is because PCM Wave audio is an uncompressed digital audio format, and it has no CPU-intensive compression algorithms applied to the data stream, and thus decoding (CPU overhead) is not an issue for telephony equipment or for CD players.

For this reason, when you start compressing digital audio assets into various file formats in Chapter 5, you can use PCM as your "baseline" file format. You probably won't put PCM into your APK file, however, because there are other formats, such as FLAC and MPEG-4 AAC, which give you the same quality using an order-of-magnitude less data.

Ultimately, the only way to find out which Android-supported audio formats have the best digital audio result for any given audio data is to actually encode digital audio in all the primary codecs that you know are well-supported and efficient. I show you how this is accomplished in Chapter 5.

Summary

In this chapter, you took a look at digital audio concepts, principles, and the Android audio file formats that compress and decompress your digital audio assets. You looked at audio sound waves, frequency, amplitude, sampling, sample resolution, and bit-rates, and how these define your digital audio assets.

In the next chapter, you will learn about **digital audio data footprint optimization** concepts, terms, and principles.

■ ■ ■

CHAPTER 5

Digital Audio Assets: Data Footprint Optimization

You now have an understanding of the fundamental concepts, terms, and principles of digital audio new media content and the file formats that Android Studio and the Android OS support. So it's time to get into digital audio data footprint optimization and getting the smallest possible digital audio file size for your audio assets while also getting high-quality audio playback.

You will look at the open source Audacity 2.1.1 software package and learn how it can be used to record, edit, enhance, compress, and optimize digital audio assets, as you take the analog and digital waveform concepts that you learned in Chapter 4, and apply them to Android Studio.

You'll look at primary considerations for optimizing your Android digital audio assets (including device compatibility), a baseline asset to gauge compression against, and at each codec.

Audio Optimization: Device Compatibility

Optimizing your digital audio assets for playback across the widest range of Android devices in the marketplace is going to be easier than optimizing digital video or digital imagery. This is because there is a much wider disparity of screen resolutions and display aspect ratios than there is a disparity of digital audio playback hardware support, except for Android hardware featuring new 24-bit HD audio playback compatibility.

A person's ears can't perceive the quality difference in digital audio that the eyes can in digital images. There are two important "sweet spots" for digital audio support across Android devices that you should target. A lower-quality audio (narration tracks, short sound effects) can use an 11 kHz or 22 kHz sampling rate, with 8-bit, 12-bit, or 16-bit sampling resolution. High-quality audio targets include CD or HD quality audio using 16-bit or 24-bit resolution at a 48 kHz sample rate.

Your logical work process for optimizing a digital audio asset across Android devices involves creating a 16-bit asset, because all Android devices support 16-bit audio. You'll use a sample rate of 48 kHz so that you have a high-quality uncompressed starting point, and then optimize (compress) the PCM format with all the different codecs supported in Android.

Once that work process is completed, you will be able to ascertain which resulting digital audio assets provide you with the highest quality digital audio playback in conjunction with the lowest possible data footprint. Let's get right to it!

Digital Audio Optimization: Work Process

Let's launch **Audacity 2.1.1** by clicking the Quick Launch icon on your taskbar. Click the **Sampling Frequency** drop-down menu located at the bottom left of Audacity. This is shown in use in Figure 5-1; as you can see, I selected a 48 kHz sample rate. Next to the sample rate selector are settings for Snap To, and hours, minutes, seconds, and milliseconds displays for Selection Start, End, or Length and Audio Position, for micro-fine-tuning.

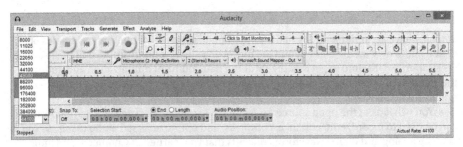

Figure 5-1. *Set a sampling rate to 48 kHz in the drop-down menu*

Now you are ready to record your voice-over. I recorded a phrase using the name of this book, *Android Studio New Media Fundamentals*. The way that you record audio in Audacity 2.1 is to click the Record button (a red dot on the right side of the Audacity transport, at the top left of the program), as shown in Figure 5-1. Speak your voice-overs into your desktop microphone; I used a Logitech stand microphone that I purchased at Walmart, originally to use in Skype, for just a few dollars.

Using a "consumer" microphone would introduce **background noise** issues, but this gives me the opportunity to show you some of the professional-level features of Audacity 2.1, such as **noise reduction**. Prepare to be amazed. I included the recording of my voice in the **Chapter5.wav** file included with this book, in case you don't have a microphone and just want to follow along.

I suggest you practice using Audacity to record your own phrase, however. In any event, once you've recorded your voice, you see a **Left and Right channel waveform** displayed inside Audacity, as shown in the center of Figure 5-2.

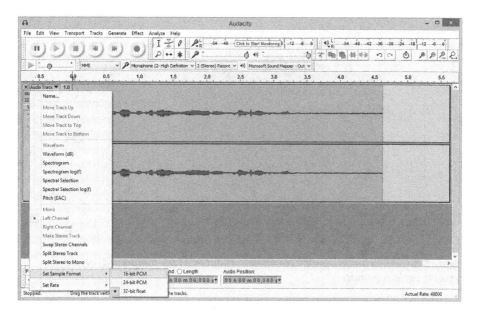

Figure 5-2. *Click the Audio Track drop-down menu; select Set Sample Format ➤ 16-bit PCM to convert 32-bit resolution to 16-bit*

Since you set the sample rate to 48 kHz before recording the vocal track, you now need to set the sample resolution from the 32-bit setting that Audacity utilizes to record. This gives you the greatest amount of data resolution to work with; it is displayed by selecting the **Audio Track ➤ Set Sample Format ➤ 32-bit float** setting, as shown in Figure 5-2.

Your first step in this data footprint optimization work process is to change the raw audio sample data format from 32-bit 48 kHz to a 16-bit 48 kHz raw audio sample data format, which is what you are using for our PCM WAV format baseline.

In Figure 5-2, this is shown in the bottom-left portion of the screen. Select **16-bit PCM** as the sample format option (instead of the 32-bit float option that Audacity set as its default) in the **Set Sample Format** submenu.

This reduces the amount of audio data going into the encoder by 100% right off the bat! You want to set a reasonable 16-bit 48 kHz audio data baseline so that you can see a compression result for each format relative to the uncompressed PCM result.

Trim an Audio Sample: Removing Unused Audio

The next thing that you need to do to reduce the overall data footprint is remove any extra audio data that is not a part of the voice-over sample. This data is usually before you start speaking and after you finish, before you hit the Stop button to end the recording function. To do this, use the vertical bar (select audio) tool at the right side of your Transport buttons to select only the relevant audio data, as shown in Figure 5-3.

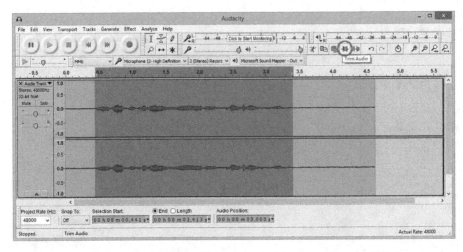

Figure 5-3. *Setting audio sample resolution to 16-bit PCM (uncompressed) before you export to various formats*

Now you are ready to use the Audacity **Trim** feature, used to trim away unused audio data. The icon that you want to click to trim away the unselected (unused) portion of your sample is shown circled in Figure 5-3, along with its tool-tip pop-up.

This provides only your vocal phrase audio portion, and you will probably have enough room in your display to zoom into the audio waveform so that you can see what you're working on with greater accuracy.

The **magnifying glass zoom tool** is right under the select tool; it is a vertical bar that looks like a text-insertion cursor. Select the zoom tool and click the waveform to zoom into it. You can resize the Audacity window toward your right to show the end of the audio sample so that you can see the entire waveform, as I did in Figure 5-4.

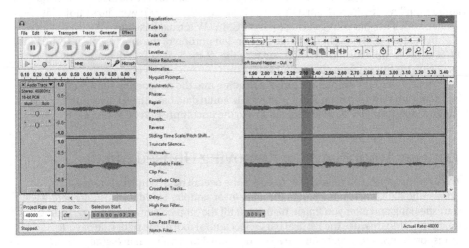

Figure 5-4. *Select an area with only noise and use the Effect ➤ Noise Reduction menu sequence*

To listen to your trimmed waveform, click the Play icon, located in the transport. This is a green right-facing arrow on the left side of the record-and-playback transport UI panel that controls what your audio does as you are working on it.

Noise Reduction: Removing Background Noise

As you play back the digital audio sample, you hear noticeable background noise that is not professional enough to have in your Android Studio application. Let's get some experience in using the Audacity **Effect** menu to remove background noise.

The work process for removing noise in Audacity—perfect for use with voice-over tracks—is to use the **vertical bar** tool select a portion of the audio sample that has only noise in it. The Noise Reduction algorithm uses this data to ascertain what data to remove from the entire audio sample in the second step of its noise removal work process.

As you can see in Figure 5-4, I've selected a section of the sample data that has noise in it but no vocal content. Then I selected the Audacity **Effect** menu ➤ **Noise Reduction** option.

This opens the Noise Reduction dialog shown in Figure 5-5, where you can click the **Get Noise Profile** button.

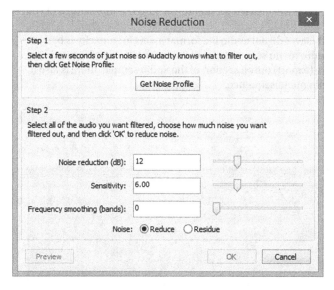

Figure 5-5. *Click the Get Noise Profile button in the Noise Reduction dialog, and then apply the algorithm by clicking OK*

Here you enter your selected noise-only data (see Figure 5-4) and pass this data to the Noise Reduction algorithm as step 1 of a noise reduction work process outlined for you in the Noise Reduction dialog.

It's important to note that even though the dialog tells you to select a "few seconds" of noise data, you don't have that much noise, so you are selecting a tenth of a second, which works just as well, as a tenth of a second of digital audio contains a significant amount of data. If you have long samples, such as reading a paragraph, you could select a couple seconds.

Alternately, you could have applied Noise Reduction before executing the Trim operation, giving you plenty more unused noise data at the beginning and end of the audio sample.

Once you click the **Get Noise Profile** button, which gives the Noise Reduction algorithm the data it needs to process, the OK button becomes enabled. You then proceed to step 2, which actually processes the noise data and removes it from your vocal audio sample entirely. The Audacity Effect feature (more of a filter, really) alone is worth the cost of Audacity. Wait a minute—Audacity is free! Sorry about that, I forgot.

Establishing a Baseline: Exporting PCM Format

The next step in the work process is to export your "baseline" 16-bit uncompressed PCM codec format as a WAV audio (.wav) file (Windows) or an AIFF audio file (Macintosh). You'll use this to see what the largest possible audio file size is, to use as the baseline, and to see how much system memory will be used for this 16-bit 48 kHz audio sample of your 3.45-seconds voice-over.

The way that you export (save) digital audio file format assets in Audacity is by selecting a **File ➤ Export Audio** menu sequence, as seen on the left side of Figure 5-6. If you want to select and save (export) only a section of the audio sample, there is also a **File ➤ Export Selected Audio** menu sequence.

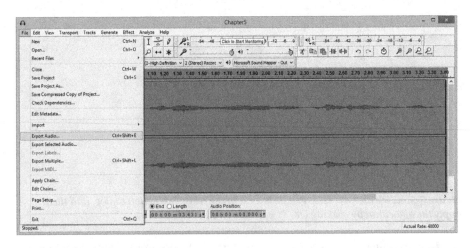

Figure 5-6. *Use the File ➤ Export Audio menu sequence to export*

The Export Selected Audio feature is quite handy if your audio sample contains audio "snippets" that you wish to extract from a longer audio data sample. In this case, you can use this feature to extract each individual word from the complete vocal.

The **Export Audio** dialog is seen in Figure 5-7, featuring key areas for name, options, file location, and codec selection.

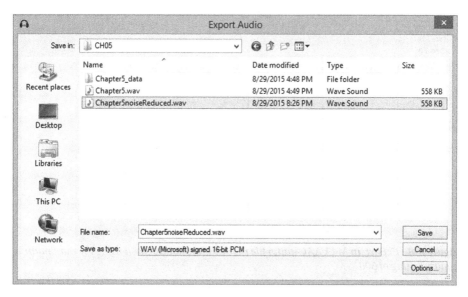

Figure 5-7. *Export a PCM file named Chapter5noiseReduced.wav to use as a baseline to measure other codec compression results*

The **Save in** folder specifier, which I have pointing to a CH05 book assets folder, tells Audacity where I want to save an audio asset. The **File List Pane**, shows the folder contents. The **File name** data entry field is where you name your file; in this case, Chapter5noiseReduced.wav. Underneath that is the **Save as type** drop-down selector, which contains all the file formats that Audacity exports to.

For this drop-down to give you all the codec formats that are supported in Android Studio, you need to have the most current LAME and FFmpeg codec libraries installed on your system so that Audacity can locate them on start-up.

Notice that I have the **Export File** dialog set to export **Chapter5noiseReduced. wav** in WAV (Microsoft) signed 16-bit PCM format. You do not need to specify the .wav extension part for the file name if you don't want to, due to the codec specifier.

If you click your **Options** button, which is located in the bottom-right corner of the **Export Audio** dialog, you'll find that for WAV audio format you'll get a dialog that informs you that there is **No encoding** option for PCM files. This is because PCM contains uncompressed data, so there are no options to set.

Once you click the **Save** button, the **Edit Metadata** dialog appears for you to enter any metadata that you want included in your audio file (see Figure 5-8). This data is stored in each file format along with the audio data; it can be accessed by Android. This dialog appears for each audio format's export.

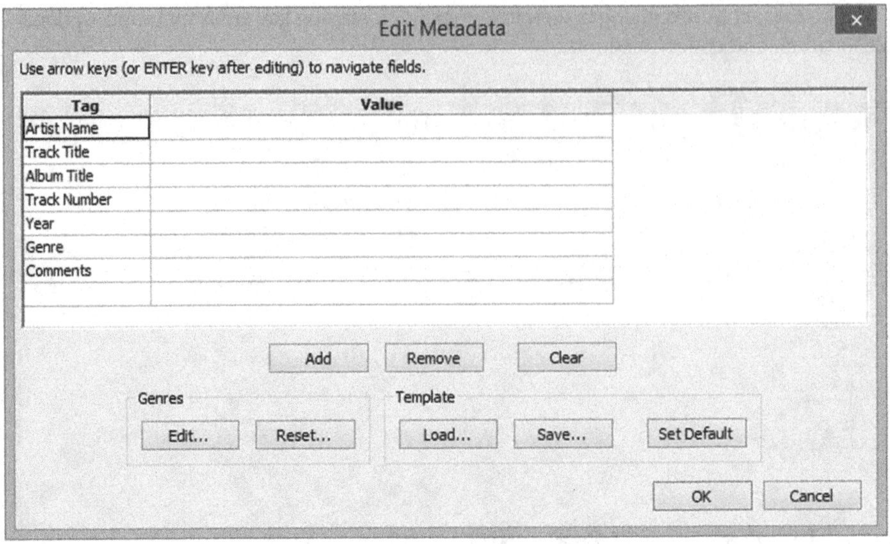

Figure 5-8. *Export an M4A AAC audio file named buttonaudio.m4a using the maximum quality setting of 500*

This dialog has data fields to contain text values, such as Artist Name, Track Title, Album Title, Track Number, Year, Genre, and Comments.

Since I'm optimizing for a baseline data footprint, and the application doesn't require audio metadata, I'm leaving these fields blank for now, so that you can get an accurate read on what a precise file size is; that is, one containing only the audio data. If you're wondering how Android Studio applications can read and support audio metadata, and you want to install this data in the audio file, the answer is Android's **MediaMetadataRetriever** class, which developers utilize for this very specific purpose.

If your Android application needs to use audio media metadata, you should use the **Edit Metadata** dialog along with the Android MediaMetadataRetriever class, which you can learn more about at http://developer.android.com/reference/android/media/ MediaMetadataRetriever.html.

If you look at the Chapter5noiseReduced.wav 16-bit PCM WAV file that you just saved, you see that the file size, at 558 KB, is a little bit more than half a megabyte.

So our baseline uncompressed data (and memory) footprint for this 3.45 seconds button sound effect sample is 558 KB. You can use this number to determine the amount of compression that you'll be getting in all the Android digital audio formats.

Exporting Lossless FLAC: FLAC Audio Files

The first format you are going to try out is the FLAC audio codec, because it uses lossless compression. This gives you a good idea of what kind of data footprint reduction you can get using compression that does not throw away any of the original audio data, and this gives you as perfect a result as the 16-bit PCM WAV audio does!

To do this, you'll again use the File ➤ Export Audio menu sequence, and this time, you will drop-down a **Save as type** menu, and select the **FLAC Files** format, as is shown in Figure 5-9.

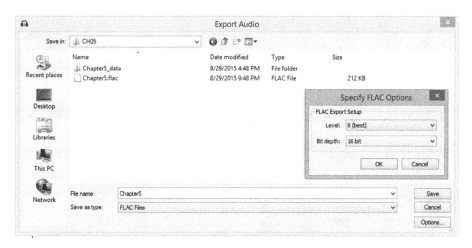

Figure 5-9. *Export a FLAC file named Chapter5.flac with Level 8 compression and a Bit depth of 16-bit*

Again, name this file Chapter5.flac. I'm going to save it into my CH05 folder for this book. Notice that there will only be FLAC files listed within your center area of this dialog. This is because now that you have selected the FLAC file format, this region in the center of your dialog only shows FLAC files, and currently there are none in the CH05 folder. Because I wanted to show a file size for each format, I saved the file prior, so the size is included in the screenshot, as well as the settings and options dialog.

To set the FLAC codec options, click the **Options** button, and set the quality **Level** to **8** (best), and the **Bit depth** to use **16-bit** data resolution. Note that under the **Bit depth** drop-down you can also use this FLAC codec for lossless, 24-bit HD audio. Notice that I am putting the Export Audio and Options dialog in one unified screen to cut down on the number of screenshots I'm using.

Once you've output your buttonaudio.flac audio asset, go into the file manager, and take a look at the file size. You will see that it is 212 KB, or reduced by over 100%. 212 ÷ 558 = 0.38, or only 38% as large as the PCM file was.

Next, let's take a look at the other open source format, Ogg Vorbis, to see if it can give us an even smaller data footprint. Since Ogg Vorbis is a lossy file format, it should provide an even smaller file size than the FLAC did.

Exporting Lossy Ogg Vorbis: OGG Audio Files

Again use the File ➤ Export Audio work process, as you have been previously to open this Export Audio dialog, and select the **Ogg Vorbis Files** option from your **Save as type** drop-down menu. I named the file Chapter5, which produces a Chapter5.ogg file name, and put it into the CH05 folder, as can be seen in Figure 5-10. Click the **Options** button, and select a **Quality** setting level between 0 and 10. I used a maximum setting of 10 to start with. During a real data footprint optimization session, you'd probably try several settings to see how the data footprint–to-quality trade-off is affected by this Quality setting slider.

Figure 5-10. *Export an OGG Vorbis file named Chapter5.ogg using a Quality level of 10*

Once you have output your Chapter5.ogg audio asset, take a look at the file size. You see that it is 149 KB, which is a 400% reduction in the file size: 149 ÷ 558 = 0.27, or roughly equal to one-fourth, or four times smaller. This is a significant size reduction, and the audio sounds the same as it did before using lossy compression at 350 out of 500, or 70% quality (350 ÷ 500=0.7).

Next, let's take a look at MP3, which is currently the most common lossy audio format. It should be quite interesting to see if MP3 can provide a smaller data footprint than the Ogg Vorbis open source codec provided of 149 KB.

Exporting Lossy MPEG-3 Format: MP3 Audio Files

Use the File ➤ Export Audio menu sequence again to bring up the Export Audio dialog and set the **Save as type** drop-down selector to **MP3 Files**, as is shown in Figure 5-11. I named the file Chapter5 and selected the CH05 folder, and then clicked the MP3 **Options** button to open the **Specify MP3 Options** dialog, which is shown on the right side of Figure 5-11. I used the maximum bit-rate **Quality** setting of 320 kbps, which is quite high for audio data, but I was trying to get a high-end baseline for MP3 compression, and still compare what MP3 can do against an uncompressed PCM baseline. I also selected **Constant Bit Rate Mode** because it is the easiest to decode, and **Stereo Channel Mode** because the file is in stereo.

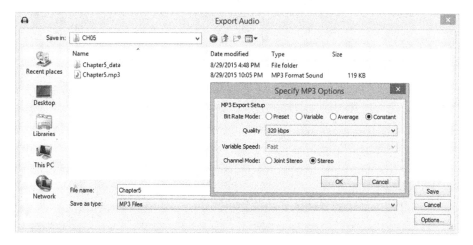

Figure 5-11. *Export an MP3 file named Chapter5.mp3 using Stereo Channel Mode, a Quality of 320 kbps and Constant Bit Rate Mode*

If you like, you can also try different Quality Bit Rate settings as well as Variable and Average Bit Rate Modes, to see how it affects the MP3 audio file data footprint. If you decide to do this, to differentiate your files from each other, simply name the file with the settings in your filename. For instance, a file with a 320 kbps Quality setting with a Variable Bit Rate Mode should be named: **Chapter6_320_kbps_vbr.mp3**, for instance.

This way, you can compare the MP3 (or any other codec file format) and audio file sizes, and do simple math to figure out your percentage data footprint reduction.

The Chapter5.mp3 file size is 119 KB, representing a 469% data footprint reduction. Let's calculate this: 119 ÷ 558 = 0.21326, which is 21% of the original, uncompressed file size; 100% – 21% = 79% file size reduction.

If you use your **1/x** (inversion) key on a calculator, you can get a percentage reduction from the other direction. Inverting 0.21326 results in 4.689, which means that you reduced the file size by 4.689 times, which equates to a 469% reduction. This is a fairly impressive data footprint reduction!

Now that you have seen that the .MP3 file size is smaller than the Ogg Vorbis, let's see how the MPEG-4 AAC in an M4A file format data compression can improve your file's size-to-quality ratio compared to MPEG-3. Since MPEG-4 uses a more advanced (and more recent) codec algorithm, M4A should provide you with a much better file size–to-quality optimization ratio.

Exporting Lossy MPEG-4 Format: M4A Audio Files

Follow the usual File ➤ Export Audio work process to invoke the Export Audio dialog and select **M4A (AAC) Files (FFmpeg)** from the **Save as type** drop-down selector. As usual, name the file Chapter5, which is named Chapter5.m4a by the Exporter after you click Save. Save it in the CH05 directory, or whatever your digital audio assets folder, and then click the **Options** button to open a **Specify AAC Options** dialog, as shown in Figure 5-12. I chose to set my Quality setting at **350**. Click **OK** to set Quality, and **Save** to export your **Chapter5.m4a** file.

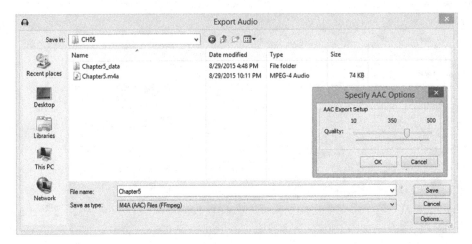

Figure 5-12. *Export an M4A file named Chapter5.m4a using a Quality of 350 out of 500*

Your Chapter5.m4a file size is 74 KB, representing 13% of an uncompressed data footprint, or an 87% reduction in data. To figure this out, 74 ÷ 558 = 0.1326, which is 13% of an original, uncompressed file size; 100% – 13% = 87% file size reduction. Invert 0.1326 and you get 7.54, or 754% data footprint reduction.

Now that you have seen that your M4A AAC file size is the most impressive data footprint reduction thus far, let's see if the much more specialized AMR-NB (Narrow Band) data compression codec gives any further data footprint improvements over MPEG-4 AAC.

Since this codec is optimized for voice, chances are the results are going to be significantly better than any that you have encountered thus far. So hold on to your hat! One thing to note about recording voice is that it does not require stereo.

Exporting Narrow Band Format: AMR Audio Files

Even though this MPEG-4 AMR-NB codec and data format was designed and optimized specifically for use for voice recording applications, there may be some other applications; for example, certain short-burst sound effects that might obtain reasonable if not great results by using this codec. As you know, any codec is simply a complex, mathematical algorithm implemented using software. It doesn't discriminate, so the only way to really find out which codec will give you the best compression-to-quality result with any given asset is to run the original uncompressed audio data through the codec and see what happens.

Let's do that next, and then you'll be finished comparing the audio codecs that are supported in Android Studio and are also available in Audacity 2.1.1. Fortunately, all the ones I would want to use for my Android applications are in Audacity.

Follow the usual File ➤ Export Audio work process, so as to invoke the Audacity Export File dialog, and then select your **AMR (narrow band) Files (FFmpeg)** option from the **Save as type** drop-down menu selector. As usual, name the file Chapter5, which is named Chapter5.amr by the Exporter after you click **Save**. Save the file in your CH05 directory, or whatever your digital audio assets folder is called, and then click the **Options** button to open the **Specify AMR-NB Options** dialog (seen on the right of Figure 5-13). I chose to use the 12.20 kbps Bit Rate setting to get the maximum quality result for this codec.

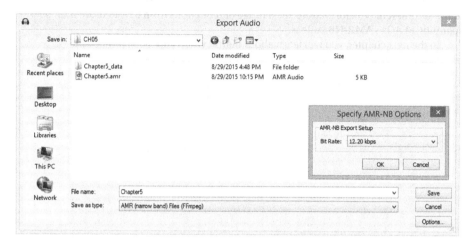

Figure 5-13. Export an AMR file named Chapter5.amr using a Bit Rate of 12.20 kbps

Click Save, and as you can see, this is the smallest data footprint that you've obtained thus far, using only 5 KB of data.

Interestingly, when you play this AMR audio sample back, it still sounds a lot like the audio contained inside the other supported codec formats that you have generated thus far.

The Chapter5.amr file size is 5 KB, representing more than a 99% data footprint reduction. Let's figure this out: 5 ÷ 558 is 0.0089 which is 0.89% of the original, uncompressed file size; 100% – 1% = 99% file size reduction. If you invert 0.00896, you get 111.6, which represents an 11,600% reduction in data footprint.

I don't know about you, but since it's only a talking app, my decision for a voice-over would be the 5 KB audio asset, rather than a 74 KB, 119 KB, 149 KB, or 212 KB audio asset.

Summary

In this chapter, you looked at digital image data footprint optimization concepts and principles regarding the six primary Android digital audio formats that can decompress your digital audio assets (created using the open source Audacity 2.1.1 professional audio editing and effects software application).

You also went over how to match the specifications for your digital audio assets to the hardware capabilities of your target Android device. For high-quality audio, this means using 24-bit 48 kHz audio for HD Audio devices, or 16-bit 48 kHz audio to cover all the Android devices out there.

You learned how to use Audacity to record audio, trim an audio clip, apply noise reduction algorithms to the stereo audio track, and export into a half-dozen of the most widely utilized digital audio codec formats used in Android Studio applications development today.

You learned how to calculate a data footprint reduction percentage, and applied this to the six different data formats, to see a range of reductions from 62% to more than 99% spanning FLAC to AMR-NB codecs.

In the next chapter, you will learn about **digital video** concepts, terms, and principles.

■ ■ ■

CHAPTER 6

Digital Video: Concepts and Terminology

Now that you have an understanding of the fundamental concepts, terms, and principles of digital audio new media content and the file format optimization for Android Studio, it is time to get into digital video new media concepts, terms, and principles. The two popular file formats that Android Studio supports are WebM and MPEG-4 AVC. You will look at the concepts behind both analog video (film) and learn how it is digitized into digital video, as many of these analog film and digital video concepts apply across both mediums.

You will look at how digital video is created using image frames displayed at a rapid rate of speed, and you will learn digital video concepts such as frame rate and resolution. You will also look at advanced digital video playback concepts, such as bit-rates, video streaming, HD audio, and captive digital video.

Finally, you'll look at open source digital video codecs and the digital video file formats supported by Android Studio, which you will use to develop Android new media applications.

Digital Video Concepts and Terminology

Digital video is comprised of both digital imagery and digital audio, which is why I covered those chapters in the first half of this book. Digital video assets use Android's digital video compatible classes, such as the **VideoView**, **MediaController**, and **MediaPlayer**. The MediaPlayer and MediaController classes are also compatible with digital audio assets, and therefore can be used for either digital audio or digital video playback.

Digital video can be used for a number of things in your Android Studio application development besides video clip playback. You can use digital video in your user interface design, in the background, or in conjunction with an i3D project design.

Digital Video Concepts: Frames and Frame Rates

Digital video extends digital images into 4D, the fourth dimension of time. This is done with something called **frames** in the digital video and film industry. A frame is simply a digital image, one that's contained in a collection of slightly different digital images, making it a digital video asset.

© Wallace Jackson 2015
W. Jackson, *Android Studio New Media Fundamentals*,
DOI 10.1007/978-1-4842-9867-1_6

Your digital video assets are comprised of an ordered sequence of frames that display rapidly and create the intended illusion of motion imagery.

The primary concept regarding frames in 2D digital video assets builds upon the primary concepts for 2D digital imaging. Digital video frames also contain **pixels**, for each image frame, which means that the digital video asset also has a **resolution**, as well as an **aspect ratio** and a **color depth**. All of the frames in your digital video asset must use the exact same resolution, aspect ratio, and color depth.

Most digital video assets use a 24-bit color depth, and this is what is supported in Android as well. Indexed color video does exist, as Microsoft Video 1 codec operates either in 8-bit palletized color mode or in a 15-bit RGB_565 color space. Animated GIF (a GIF or AnimGIF) can index the color palette for motion video graphics assets, but neither Microsoft Video 1 nor animated GIF are currently supported in the Android API.

Like pixels do in digital imagery, digital video frames multiply your data footprint with each frame used, as you will see in Chapter 7. In digital video, not only does your digital video frame's resolution greatly impact your resulting file size, but so does the number of **frames per second**, which a codec needs to analyze and compress, during the video encoding process. As you know, more data to compress equals larger file sizes, even if the compression algorithm is reducing that data.

This number of frames per second is commonly referred to as **FPS**, and is also commonly referred to as the "frame rate" in the digital video and film production industries.

Common frame rates include 60 FPS for i3D console games, 30 FPS for digital videos, 24 FPS for feature films, and 20 FPS for multimedia. As you will see in Chapter 7, there is some new media content that support lower frame rates, such as 15 FPS or 12 FPS.

To find out how long each frame is displayed, based on a frames per second (FPS) value, divide the 1 by the FPS value.

Thus, 20 FPS frames display for .05 of a second, 30 FPS frames display for .033 of a second, 24 FPS frames display for .04167 of a second, and 60 FPS for frames for .0167 of a second, and so forth. Next, let's look at the mathematics to calculate raw video data, or the amount of system memory that is needed.

Digital Video Mathematics: Doing the Multiplication

In Chapter 2, you learned that if you multiply the number of pixels in your image by the number of color channels, you get the raw data footprint for that image. With digital video, you multiply that number against the number of frames per second, which the digital video is set to play back to get the data footprint per second. To get the total data footprint, you multiply that number again by the number of seconds that represent the duration of the video clip.

So with a VGA, or SD video, with a 640×480 resolution and a 24-bit color depth, you have **[(640x480)x3]=921,600** for just one frame of video. At 30 FPS this is **921,600x30=27,648,000** bytes of data. Divide this by 1024, and you have 27,000 KB of data, or 27 MB of raw data (or system memory) for one second of video.

You can see why having a powerful video codec that compresses this raw data footprint down by an order of magnitude—given the optimal compression settings—is extremely important! Let's take a look at digital video codec algorithms next, so you can see how the codec is able to accomplish this.

Digital Video Algorithms: Digital Video Codecs

You will be amazed by some of the digital video data compression ratios that you will achieve using MPEG-4 and WebM video file formats once you know exactly how to best optimize a digital video compression work process. This is done by using the correct bit-rate, frame rate, frame resolution, and color depth for your digital video content and the specific application.

You'll be taking a hands-on approach to learning this in Chapter 7, when you create (render) 3D video content in **Terragen 3.3**, encapsulate it using an **AVI** file format, and then compress it with **Sorenson Squeeze Pro** software. So you can focus on the software in the next chapter; I try to cover all concepts and theories that apply to your digital video data footprint optimization work process in this chapter. I am doing one chapter on theory and one on using software for each new media genre.

Let's take a look at how the digital video codec differs from a digital audio or digital image codec. There are some elements of both digital image and digital audio compression in digital video compression algorithms, but it can be an order of magnitude more complex because it has to ascertain and compress **inter-frame** pixel movements. So, not only does a codec compress in 2D space (pixels and waveform), but it also compresses in 4D space; that is, any changes between frames. For this reason, talking-head videos, or video with no panning or zoom, compress better because there are pixels that don't move between frames.

Video in Android: MPEG-4 H.264 AVC and WebM

Android Studio supports the same two open source digital video formats that HTML5 supports: the MPEG-4 H.264 AVC and the ON2 VP8 and ON2 VP9 codecs, which were acquired by Google from ON2 Technologies. Google renamed these WebM, and then released them in an open source licensing schema. This is great news from a content production standpoint, as video content that developers produce and optimize could be used in HTML5 apps, browsers, and hardware devices, as well as in an Android Studio application. Android 5.0 and later also adds support for MPEG-4 H.265 HEVC (playback only).

This digital video format cross-platform support affords content developers with the "produce once, deliver everywhere," production scenario that every content producer and programmer dreams about. This could reduce content development costs, thus increasing your revenues, as long as these "economies of scale" in content development are taken advantage of by developers.

Since all Android devices these days have displays that use the medium-(1280×720) to high- (1920×1800) resolution, and some use an ultra-high (4096×2160) resolution, you would utilize the MPEG-4 H.264 AVC format. This is the digital video format most often used in the world today for Android or HTML5.

MPEG-4 H.264 AVC: The Most Widely Used and Supported Codec

This MPEG-4 H.264 AVC (Advanced Video Coding) video file format is supported across every Android version for playback, and in Android 3.0 and later versions, for video recording.

If you are a video content producer, you will find that this MPEG-4 H.264 AVC format gives the best compression result, especially if you are using one of the more advanced encoding suites, like the Sorenson Squeeze Professional software, which you'll be using to optimize our 3D video asset in Chapter 7.

File extension support for MPEG-4 digital video includes **.3GP** (MPEG4 SP or Standard Play), and **.MP4** (MPEG4 H.264 AVC). I suggested using the latter MPEG-4 AVC, which is what I use for HTML5; MP4 is more common to stream with an AVC format, but either type of extension should work just fine in Android apps.

ON2 VP8 and VP9: The Newcomer WebM or WebMovie Format

A recent digital video format Android Studio supports is called the WebM digital video format. This format also provides high-quality results in a small data footprint. This is the reason why Google acquired ON2, which is the company that developed the VP8 and VP9 codecs. Playback of WebM video was first natively supported in Android 2.3. The term "native support" is used with API code; in this case, it's a codec that has become part of Android OS.

WebM also supports video streaming, which you'll also be learning about in a later section of this chapter. A WebM video streaming playback capability is supported on Android 4 and later versions.

For this reason, I recommend using WebM for **captive** video assets, as non-streaming WebM codec supported in Android 2.3 through 5.4.

In case you're wondering, captive video is video that is not streamed, where video assets are captive inside a /res/raw/ folder. You first encountered captive vs. streaming concepts in Chapter 3, which coves digital audio concepts and techniques.

If you're only going to stream video, use an MPEG-4 H.264 AVC, as that codec has been supported across all the Android Studio versions and all the Android API levels since 1.5.

Digital Video Resolutions: Industry Standards

Let's start out by covering the primary resolutions used in commercial video. Before HDTV (high-definition television) came along, video was called "SD," or standard definition, and used a standard vertical resolution of 480 pixels. The original aspect ratio for SD was 4:3 (640×480). More recently, a widescreen aspect ratio was added, making SD video a 720×480 resolution.

HD resolution video comes in two different resolutions: 1280×720, which I call "pseudo HD," and 1920×1080, which the video industry calls "true HD." Both use a 16:9 widescreen aspect ratio, and are now used not only in film, HD television, and iTV sets, but also in smartphones (Razor HD is 1280×720) and tablets (the Kindle Fire HD is 1920×1200).

The 1920×1200 resolution is, by the way, a less wide, or taller, 16:10 pixel aspect ratio. It is becoming more common as a widescreen device aspect ratio, as is the 16:8, or 2:1 aspect ratio, with 2160×1080 screens out in the market since 2013.

There is also 16:10 pseudo HD resolution, which features 1280×800 pixels. In fact, this is a common laptop, notebook, Netbook, and mid-size tablet resolution. I will not be surprised to see a 16:8 1280×640 screen offered at some point.

Generally, content developers try to match the video content resolution to the resolution (and thus the aspect ratio as well) of each Android device that their video asset will be viewed upon.

Similarly, manufacturers try to match display screen resolution to popular content resolutions. Blu-ray is 1280×720, and so there are a lot of 1280×720 screens and 2560×1440 screen sizes (two times 1280×720 on each axis scales up perfectly with a 4-pixel (2x2) matrix, for each pixel in the Blu-ray content.

Digital Video Storage: Captive vs. Streaming

Regardless of the resolution you choose for your digital video content, video can be accessed by an Android Studio application in a couple of different ways. The way I do it, because I am a data optimization freak, is captive within an application. This means the data is inside of the Android application's APK file itself, inside of the /res/raw/ raw data resource folder.

The other way to access video inside your Android app is by using a remote video data server. In this case, the video is streamed from the remote server, over the Internet, and to your user's Android device as the video plays in real time. Let's hope your video server doesn't crash, which is one of the downsides of streaming video, relative to captive video.

Video streaming is inherently more complicated than playing captive digital video. This is because the Android device is communicating in real time with a remote data server, receiving video data packets, decoding the data packets as the video plays, and then writing the frames to an Android hardware display. Video streaming is supported via WebM on Android 4 and later devices using the WebM format, or by using MPEG-4 on all Android OS versions.

Digital Video Compression: Bit Rates and Playback

Another important digital video concept that you need to learn is **bit-rates**. A bit-rate is a key setting used in the video compression process, as you will see when you utilize Sorenson Squeeze Pro 10 in Chapter 7. Bit-rates represent the **target bandwidth**, or the **data pipe size**, that is able to accommodate a certain number of data bits that stream through it every second. Bit-rates also need to take into consideration the CPU processing power within any given Android phone, making video data optimization even more important to your Android Studio application's playback quality.

This is because once the bits travel through a data pipe, they also need to be processed and then displayed on the device screen. In fact, captive video assets included in Android APK files, *only* need optimizations for processing power. The reason for this is because if you are using captive video files, there is no data pipe for the video asset to travel through, and thus no data transfer overhead. So the bit-rate for digital video assets needs to be optimized not only for data bandwidth but also with an anticipation of variances in CPU capability.

In general, the smaller the video data file size, the faster the data will travel through a data pipe, the easier to decode that data using the codec and the CPU, and the smaller the Android APK file size.

Single-core CPUs in devices such as smartwatches may not be able to decode high-resolution, high bit-rate digital video assets without "dropping" frames. This is a playback quality issue, so make sure to thoroughly optimize lower bit-rate video assets if you are going to target older (or cheaper) devices.

Digital Video Optimization: Encoding Software

I will go over digital video optimization theory in the last part of the chapter so you can focus on work process and software during Chapter 7. The **decoder** side of your digital video codec is always optimized for speed, because smoothness of playback is the key issue; the encoder side is optimized to reduce the data footprint for the digital video asset that it is generating. For this reason, an encoding process may take a long time, depending on how many processing cores a workstation contains. Most video content production workstations should support eight, twelve, or sixteen processor cores, so that encoding is faster and special effects are rendered quickly.

Codecs on an **encoder** side are like plug-ins in the sense that they can be installed into different digital video editing software packages to encode different digital video asset file formats. Since the Android OS supports H.263, H.264 and H.265 MPEG-4 formats and ON2 VP8 and VP8 WebM formats for video, you need to make sure that you're using one of these codecs that encodes video data into digital video file formats.

More than one software manufacturer makes MPEG4 encoding software, so there is MPEG codec encoder software that yields different (better or worse) results, as far as encoding speed and file size goes.

If you wish to encode digital video assets, I recommend professional encoding solution Sorenson Squeeze Pro from Sorenson Media, which is currently at version 10.

Squeeze has a professional-level version, which I will use in this book; it costs about $1,000, but its value is in excess of the suggested list price if you consider what it can do. There are also less expensive versions of the software that are available.

There is also an open source solution called Editshare Lightworks 12.5, but the free version does not currently support output using an MPEG-4 AVC and WebM VP8 or VP9 codecs; although the WebM codec is open sourced, so that support could potentially be added. So I'll have to use Sorenson Squeeze Pro 10 for the book. (Perhaps the codec support for Android Studio and HTML5 will be added to Editshare Lightworks 12.5, or later. Visit the Lightworks forum—users are requesting WebM support be added to Lightworks).

Digital Video Optimization: Encoder Settings

When optimizing for digital video asset file size using encoder settings, there are a number of important settings that directly affect a data footprint. I'll cover these in the order in which they affect the file size, from the most impact to the least impact, so you know which parameters to "tweak" or adjust to obtain the results that you're looking for. As with digital image compression, the resolution, or number of pixels in each frame of video is the optimal place to start your data optimization process. If you are targeting 1280×720 smartphones or tablets, you do not need to use 1920×1080 resolution to get great visual results from your digital video assets.

With high density, also termed "fine dot-pitch" displays (Android's HDPI, XHDPI, XXHDPI, and XXXHDPI) currently common in the Android market, you can scale up 1280 video by 33% and it will look reasonably good. The exception to this is iTV apps on Android TV, which has a medium MDPI dot pitch due to large 55- to 95- inch screen sizes. If you are developing applications for iTV sets, you want to use a 1920×1080 "true HD" resolution so that your content hits every pixel. This can be scaled up to 3840×2160, to support UHD with good results.

The next level of optimization comes in the number of frames used for each second of video (FPS). This assumes the actual seconds contained in the video itself can't be shortened through editing. This is known as the frame rate; so instead of setting a video standard 30 FPS frame rate, consider using the film standard frame rate of 24 FPS, or the multimedia standard frame rate of 20 FPS. You may be able to use a low 15 FPS frame rate, depending upon your content.

Note that 15 FPS is half as much source data as 30 FPS, which is a 100% reduction of data going into the encoder. For some video content, this plays back the same as 30 FPS content. The only reliable way to test how low you can get the FPS before it starts to affect your video playback quality is to set, encode, and review the result with different frame rate settings during your digital video (encoder) content optimization work process.

The next optimal setting to tweak or experiment with to obtain a smaller data footprint is the bit-rate for a codec. Bit-rate settings equate to the amount of compression applied, and thus set the visual quality for video data. It is important to note that you could simply use 30 FPS, HD 1920×1080 video and specify a low bit-rate ceiling. If you do this, however, the results would not look as good as if you first experimented with lower frame rates and resolutions using the higher (quality) bit-rate settings.

The next most effective setting in obtaining a small data footprint is the number of keyframes. The codec uses your keyframe settings to know when to sample the digital video. Video codecs apply compression by looking at a frame, and then encoding only the changes, or offsets, over the next few frames so that it does not have to encode every single frame in the video data stream. This is why a talking-head video encodes better than a video where every pixel moves on every frame, such as video with fast panning or rapid zooming, for instance.

The keyframe setting in the encoder forces the codec to take a fresh frame sample of a video data asset every so often. There is usually an auto setting for keyframes; this allows the codec to decide the number of keyframes to sample. There is also a manual setting that allows you to specify a keyframe sampling every so often, usually a certain number of times per second, or a certain number of times over the duration of the video (total frames).

The next most effective setting in obtaining a small data footprint is the quality or the sharpness setting, which is usually implemented using a slider. Sharpness controls the amount of blur that the codec applies to the video pixels before compression. In case you are wondering how this trick works so that you can apply it in GIMP during your own digital image optimization work process, applying a slight blur to your image or video, which is usually not desirable, allows better compression. The reason for this is that a sharp transition in an image (such as sharp edges between colors) is more difficult for the codec to encode optimally; that is, it uses less data. More precisely (no pun intended), sharp or abrupt transitions in color take more data to reproduce than soft transitions do. I recommend keeping the quality or sharpness slider between an 85% and 100% quality setting, and try to get your data footprint reduction using the other variables discussed here.

Ultimately, there are a significant number of different variables that you'll need to fine-tune to achieve the best data footprint optimization for each particular video data asset. Each is different (mathematically) to the codec, as each video asset may be a different array (collection) of pixel color data. For this reason, there is no "standard" collection of settings that can be developed to achieve any given result.

Your experience tweaking various settings may eventually allow you to get a better feel of the settings you need to change to get your desired compression results.

Again, you get some hands-on experience with all of this in Chapter 7.

Summary

In this chapter, you took a look at the digital video concepts, principles, and Android formats that compress and decompress digital video assets. You looked at how resolution, color depth, frame rates, bit-rates, and codec settings can contribute to digital video asset data footprint reduction.

In the next chapter, you will learn about **digital video data footprint optimization** using popular software packages.

■ ■ ■

CHAPTER 7

Digital Video Assets: Data Footprint Optimization

Now that you have an understanding of the fundamental concepts, terms, and principles of digital video new media content and the digital video asset optimization considerations for the two primary codecs that are supported in Android Studio, it is time to get into the work process for creating, encoding, and optimizing a digital video asset from scratch using the popular software packages Terragen, VirtualDub, and Squeeze.

Since 3D-rendered content is more "orderly" because it's created by algorithms (math) rather than random CCD data, it'll compress better. Plus, I can show you how to create 2D video content out of "thin air." I can also show you a complex workflow involving multiple software packages, most of them open source. You can substitute Lightworks for Squeeze for 100% open sourced workflow, if you prefer.

Creating Digital Video Content: Terragen

You need to learn how to create digital video content from scratch, as well as how to optimize its data footprint. To do this, I am going to use Terragen 3.3, a world-creation 3D animation software package from Planetside Software; it is not only an impressive 3D software package, but it is also a professional-level 3D production software package. Fortunately, there is a free version, as well as a paid Pro version that I suggest you purchase if you are serious about having all the best production tools in your toolkit. Go to the web site at **planetside.co.uk**, shown in Figure 7-1, and download the latest version of Terragen 3. After you download and install the software, launch it with a shortcut icon. You see the Credits and Support tabs, also shown in Figure 7-1, in the various rendered start-up screens for the software. You can see exactly what this software is capable of by viewing these different start-up screens; they are truly magnificent.

© Wallace Jackson 2015
W. Jackson, *Android Studio New Media Fundamentals*,
DOI 10.1007/978-1-4842-9867-1_7

Figure 7-1. Using Terragen 3.3 to create video (credits screen)

As you can see, this software package rocks in the hands of the seasoned user! Next, so that you don't have to learn all the intricacies of Terragen, open a seamless looping 3D camera fly-over of a virtual world, which you'll find in the book assets folder named **loopingOrbit_v03.tgd**.

A .tgd file is a **TerraGen Data** format file; it contains native Terragen projects. You should use Terragen's **File ➤ Open** menu sequence to open these types of files in your Terragen 3.3 software package.

Once you open this file, you should see the Terragen 3.3 software package, with areas for 3D world creation preview, and panes for settings and visual programming (shown in Figure 7-2).

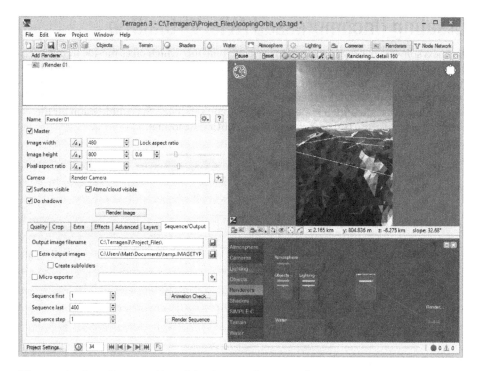

Figure 7-2. *Start Terragen: Use File ➤ Open on loopingOrbit_v03*

In the top part of your render dialog (shown on the left), set an image width of 480 pixels, and an image height of 800 pixels. This is one of the more popular Android hardware device resolutions. The WVGA resolution has enough pixels to scale up or down with good results. Leave all the other render settings at their default settings.

If you just want to render a single frame, you could use the **Render Image** button, seen in the middle of this dialog, but this will not create a sequence of frames, which you need to create motion video data. At the bottom of this dialog, you see seven tabs, which control your advanced settings.

Click your seventh (rightmost) tab, which is labeled **Sequence/Output**, to set the **output file specifications** as well as the **image sequence settings**.

Enter your project files directory, in your **Output image filename** field, as shown in Figure 7-2. As you can see in the screenshot, mine is named C:\Terragen3\Project_Files. Make sure that your **Sequence first** field is set to a value of **1**, and then set a value of **400** in your **Sequence last** field.

Set your Sequence step to **1 frame**. Once you have set all of your parameters for your render, click your **Render Sequence** button, which instructs Terragen to generate 400 frames of custom digital video fly-over for you.

Since Terragen outputs numbered BMP files instead of the AVI format that Squeeze requires, you need to learn about a cool software utility called VirtualDub. Next, you will utilize a VirtualDub workflow that allows you to generate an AVI file that is termed in the digital video industry as being "full frames uncompressed."

Creating Uncompressed AVIs: VirtualDub

The next software package you need to use is **VirtualDub**, which takes the 400 frames you created in Terragen and loads them into an AVI file format. Then you can import the AVI in Squeeze for the compression work process. Download and install VirtualDub from **www.virtualdub.org** and then launch it. You see an empty screen (shown in Figure 7-3), where you can use the **Video ➤ Compression** menu sequence. Set compression for the resulting file to use the **Uncompressed RGB/YCbCr** data format.

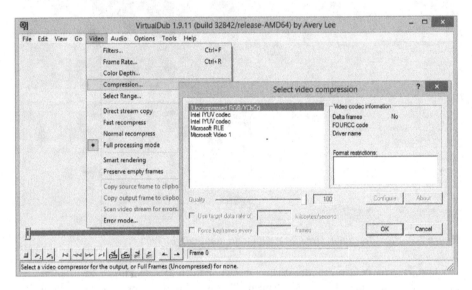

Figure 7-3. Launch VirtualDub and use Video ➤ Compression menu

Select the **Video ➤ Frame Rate**, **Video ➤ Color Depth** and the **Video ➤ Select Range** menu sequences to set the compression parameters to **10 FPS, 24-bit color**, and **0 to 400**, respectively, as seen in the series of dialogs shown in Figure 7-4.

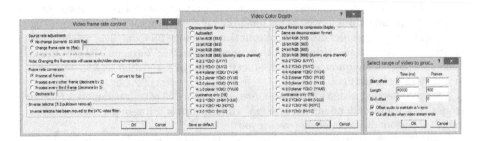

Figure 7-4. Setting the frame rate, video color depth, and frame range for an uncompressed AVI digital video data file

Now you are ready to load the 400 numbered BMP frames (shown in Figure 7-5) using the **File ➤ Open** file menu sequence.

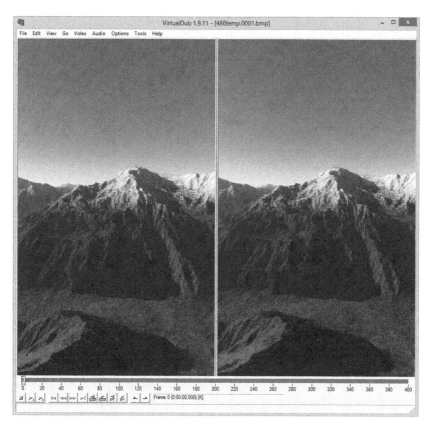

Figure 7-5. *Use File ➤ Open to open the first frame in a 400-frame 3D rendering sequence of numbered BMP files*

Select the first frame in the 400 frame BMP sequence and click the **Open** button to open all 400 frames in VirtualDub. You will see Frame 0 displayed in the software, once all 400 frames have loaded. There should be a 400-frame duration timeline located at the bottom, as shown in Figure 7-5.

Next, use the **File ➤ Save AVI 2.0 File** menu sequence to open the dialog shown in Figure 7-6. Name the file whatever you want (I used intro.avi), and then use the **Save** button to save the AVI file to your hard disk drive (I created an AVIs folder).

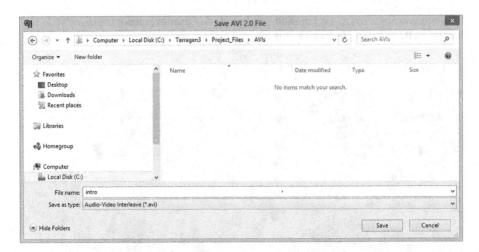

Figure 7-6. *Use the File ➤ Save AVI 2.0 File dialog to save an uncompressed AVI file in a Terragen3/Project_Files/AVIs folder*

After you click the Save button, you see the AVI building processing start. I call this a "building" process and not a compression process because the AVI that you are creating is a full-frame uncompressed digital video file format; thus there is no compression, simply placement of numbered BMP files in what appears to be a digital video file format to Squeeze, so it imports this data for compression.

A real-time progress dialog is shown in VirtualDub (see Figure 7-7) as the frame buffer is written (not compressed) into the AVI file container.

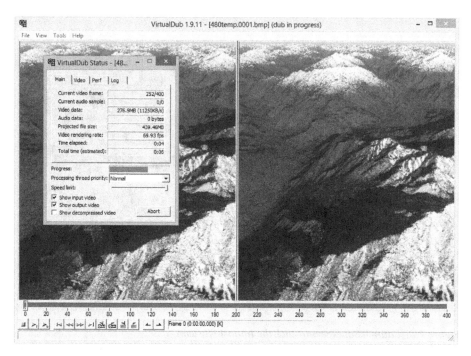

Figure 7-7. *VirtualDub loads 400 frames into a full-frames uncompressed AVI format while showing the build progress*

The reason you are using an uncompressed AVI file is twofold. First of all, this is a format that Sorenson Squeeze is able to read. Squeeze does not currently support reading numbered files, which must make 3D animators scratch their heads in disbelief.

More importantly, you want to give your codec uncompressed (raw) pristine data in order to get the optimal visual quality–to–file size trade-off result.

Now that you have 400 frames of digital video data in an AVI format that Squeeze can import, you can launch Squeeze and proceed with your data footprint optimization work process.

Applying Video Compression: Squeeze

You're going to use Sorenson Squeeze 10 to compress our digital video asset. One of the reasons I used Terragen and VirtualDub is to create completely uncompressed source video that has zero compression artifacts. If you want to get close to the same pristine data from using a camera, you would use FireWire, capturing full-frame uncompressed (raw) video data to your hard disk drive, instead of using on-camera MPEG, or M-JPEG, compression.

Install Squeeze and launch it. Next, click the **Import File** icon in the upper-right (see Figure 7-8). Notice that the Squeeze software has left panels for holding codec, filter, and publishing options, a top preview area, and the bottom timeline area (which you'll be using soon), to apply MPEG-4 codec presets(or WebM presets if you want to use that format) to intro.avi.

71

Figure 7-8. *Launch Squeeze and click the Import File icon*

Once you click the **Import File** icon, you'll see a **Select one or more source media files to open** dialog, which uses a folder name as the dialog title; in this case, this is **AVIs**, as shown in Figure 7-9 at the top of the screenshot.

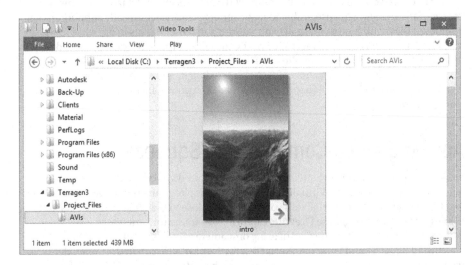

Figure 7-9. *The Import File dialog showing the intro.avi file*

If you can't find this file, navigate into the Terragen3 Project_Files subfolder, and then to your AVIs subfolder. Click your intro AVI file to select it and then click the **Select File icon**, seen in the upper-left corner of Figure 7-9 as the document icon with a red check mark inside of it. This loads an uncompressed AVI file into Sorenson Squeeze for data footprint optimization.

As you can see in Figure 7-10, on the left-hand side, the video data loads into Squeeze and displays this intro.avi file in the bottom area of the software, where you apply the codec presets once you create them, which you are going to do next.

Figure 7-10. *Squeeze showing AVI file loaded and codecs (left); right-click an MPEG-4 codec and click Edit (right)*

Click the right-facing arrow next to the MPEG-4 codecs to open the MPEG-4 codecs submenu. Right-click the **768Kbps_360p** preset, which comes with Sorenson Squeeze.

Select the **Edit** menu option so that you can edit the presets. Editing existing presets, giving them unique names, and saving them as your own customized presets is an easy way to create your own data compression setting files to use on your 480×800 intro.mp4 file, which you will create next.

This Edit context-sensitive (right-click) menu option opens the **Preset** dialog, shown in Figure 7-11. You can use the dialog to set the different compression options, which you learned about in Chapter 6.

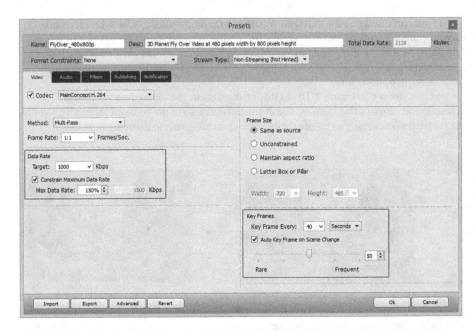

Figure 7-11. Showing MPEG-4 codec settings for 3D fly-over at 480x800 and 1000Kbps

First, let's name the preset **FlyOver_480x800p** and enter a description, **3D Planet Fly Over Video at 480 pixels width by 800 pixels height**, at the top of the dialog.

Make sure that your **Stream Type** is set to **Non-Streaming**, since the video is going to be in an Android Studio app folder. **Format Constraints** should be set to **None**.

Select the **MainConcept** H.264 MPEG-4 encoder by selecting and then using the **Codec** drop-down menu. Using the **Method** drop-down menu, select a **Multi-Pass** compression algorithm approach.

Multiple passes should certainly take the longest amount of time to compress your digital video content; however, using this setting also yields the finest compression-to-quality ratio result possible using this encoder's algorithms.

Leave the Frame Rate drop-down at 1:1 so that each frame is included in the target digital video asset, and then set the target **Data Rate** to **1000** Kbps.

Select the **Constrain Maximum Date Rate** check box. Set a **Max Data Rate** of **150%**, which gives you a bit-rate ceiling of **1500** Kbps.

On the right side of the Presets dialog, set **Frame Size** to match the source AVI resolution of 480×800 by selecting the **Same as source** option.

In the Key Frames area in the bottom right of the dialog, set the **Key Frame Every** drop-down to **40** seconds, as this is your duration for the 400-frame video that is compressed in VirtualDub, at **10 FPS**. This yields a 40-second duration.

Also, be sure to select the **Auto Key Frame on Scene Change** option. This allows the MainConcept codec to determine when to take a new data sample; that is, a keyframe of your digital video frame data. Since a video codec looks at "deltas" between frames—that is, which pixels have moved from one frame to the next, sampling new keyframe data improves quality. But it also may increase your data footprint since frame image data is stored so that the frames that follow it can later be re-created.

The reason you are selecting the auto keyframe option is to allow the MainConcept codec to decide, algorithmically, the optimal number of keyframe samples to take during a compression pass. When everything is set correctly, click the **OK** button.

As you can see at the bottom of Figure 7-12, this preset has been added underneath your Source intro.avi. You can now right-click the preset, shown on the left side of Figure 7-12, and select the **Apply Preset** option from the context menu, which adds this compression preset to your Squeeze project.

Figure 7-12. *Right-click and Apply Preset (left), showing applied preset (center), Ready to Compress message (right)*

Once you've applied the preset to your intro.avi file, as shown in Figure 7-12, you can click the **Squeeze It!** button and create the MPEG-4 file by using the codec preset that you just designed. The file name includes your source file name plus the codec preset name. This is so that if you change the preset settings, you'll be sure to get different resulting file names.

Use the uncompressed AVI file in the same way that you used the PCM WAV file as a baseline; and do the same math to find the percentage by which you have reduced the data footprint.

Be sure to look at the quality level in the video playback as well, and then adjust those codec settings, such as Bit-Rates, Keyframe Samples, and Frame Rates, until your visual quality starts to visibly suffer due to the introduction of motion pixel artifacts.

This is the point in your work process at which you have the maximum possible data footprint reduction (optimization) for your digital video asset. Any further reductions required by your Android Studio application will have to be achieved by reducing the resolution of the source AVI file.

Summary

In this chapter, you took a look at the work process for digital video data footprint optimization using several popular software packages, including Planetside Software Terragen 3.3, VirtualDub 1.9.11, and Sorenson Squeeze Pro Desktop 10.

You created a 3D virtual world fly-over using Terragen 3, and then created a source AVI using VirtualDub, and then used the professional Sorenson Squeeze Pro Desktop 10 software to create an MPEG-4 H.264 AVC file that can be used in Android Studio.

You looked at how the source video resolution, keyframes, aspect ratio, frame rate, bit-rate, and auto-keyframe settings can be set using the codec presets dialog, and how they should contribute to the digital video asset data footprint reduction.

In the next chapter, you will learn more about **digital illustration concepts and terminology** using popular software packages.

■ ■ ■

CHAPTER 8

Digital Illustration: Concepts and Terminology

Now that you have an understanding of the fundamental concepts, terminology, principles, and data footprint optimization for your digital imagery, digital audio, and digital video new media content for Android Studio, it's time to get into the areas of 2D and 3D vector new media. Android Studio only supports one open source 2D vector format, called **SVG**, or **Scalable Vector Graphics**, so that makes things easy. In this chapter, you can focus on concepts and terminology, and then on creating and optimizing scalable vector graphics assets in the next chapter. In Chapter 10, you can take 2D vector imagery into the third dimension by looking at 3D vector imagery.

In this chapter, you'll look at how digital illustration is created, using points in 2D space, lines and curves connecting those points to create shapes, and color fills, gradients, and patterns inside of these 2D vector shapes. You will also look at the open source digital illustration SVG data file format that is supported by Android Studio, as well as other open platforms, such as Java and HTML5.

Digital Illustration Is Rendered, Not Stored

As you learned in Chapter 2, pixel-based digital imagery is technically called **raster imagery**, because an array of pixel values is rasterized to a screen, displaying the image created using these pixels. Digital illustration, or **vector imagery**, is not stored as an array of image elements (pixels); instead, it's drawn or "rendered" to the screen, just like you would draw it if someone was watching you draw, only with instructions that the computer uses to do exactly what you did when you created it. This is the equivalent of the MIDI concept you learned about in Chapter 4, where the performance (in that case, it was composing music) is re-created by the computer processor, which renders it to the screen (SVG) or synthesizer (MIDI) using playback instructions.

With vector images this is accomplished with coordinates in the 2D X,Y space along with mathematics that define curves, and conveyed using SVG instructions that look a lot like code. You need to learn the basic constructs of vector illustration first, however, so that you understand how it all goes together. After that, you will look at how the SVG format turns these into instructions, which can be processed in Android Studio, by using Java or JavaFX SVG –compatible classes. SVG can also be processed by HTML5 devices.

© Wallace Jackson 2015
W. Jackson, *Android Studio New Media Fundamentals*,
DOI 10.1007/978-1-4842-9867-1_8

Vector Components: Vertices and Curves

Digital illustration vector images are composed of **points** using **coordinates** in 2D space, and **lines** or **curves** that connect those points together. You will look at concepts and terminology for these points and lines in this section. If you create a "closed" shape, that is, one where there are no openings, for a **fill** (color, pattern, or gradient) to escape, you can also fill a vector shape, so that the shape looks solid instead of empty.

The Vertex: The Foundation for Your 2D Shapes

The foundation for any 2D or 3D vector asset is called a **vertex**. Multiple vertices are required to create a line or **arc**, which require two vertices, or a **closed shape**, which requires at least three vertices. Vertices are used in both 2D vector (SVG) data processing, as well as in 3D vector (OpenGL ES) data processing, both of which are integrated into Android Studio.

Vertex data is outlined in SVG using **X,Y coordinates**, as you might have guessed, which tell the processor where a vertex is located in a 2D space. Without these vertex coordinates, the lines and the curves cannot be drawn because they must have an **origin** and a **destination** vertex coordinate as part of the line drawing operation. A line and an arc are examples of an **open shape**.

When you get into creating and looking at SVG data, you'll notice that these X,Y numeric pairs are the majority of the SVG data, which can be contained using the XML format, or in a Java SVG object for an Android Studio application. SVG data can also be used in your JavaScript (HTML5) code, as well as in JavaFX (Java 8 or Java 9) code, so it is compatible across each of your open platform application development work flows.

An X,Y coordinate all by its lonesome is what is termed one dimensional, or **1D**. (Make sure not to use this term around your spouse, and if you do, make sure it references something other than your spouse.) It takes two vertex coordinates to be considered two dimensional, or 2D; so a line or a curve (open shapes), or a closed shape is a 2D object.

The Path: Connecting Vertices to Create a Shape

A path is defined in SVG using a "path" data element. Both an open shape and a closed shape are technically a path according to the SVG specification. An SVG path represents the outline of an open or closed shape that can be filled or stroked, or used as a clipping path. These concepts are covered in detail in the chapter, but a **fill** deals with the interior of a path, a **stroke** deals with the lines or curves that make up a path, and a **clipping path** is used for Boolean operations.

In SVG data, an SVG Path object represents 2D "geometry" used to outline a Path object. In fact, in JavaFX, the class is actually called the **SVGPath** class. SVG path data can be defined in terms of SVG commands, which I outline later in the chapter using Table 8-1. Some of these include a **moveto** command, which sets your current point; a **lineto** command, which draws straight lines; a **curveto** command, which draws **cubic Bézier** curves; the **elliptical arc** command, which draws an elliptical arc; and the **closepath** command, which closes a current shape, drawing a line to its starting point. There are also advanced SVG commands.

Table 8-1. *SVG Commands to Use for Creating SVG Path Data*

SVG Command	Symbol	Type	Parameter	Description
moveto	M	Absolute	X, Y	Defines a Start Of Path at the X,Y using absolute coordinates
moveto	M	Relative	X, Y	Defines a Start Of Path at the X,Y using relative coordinates
closepath	Z	Absolute	None	Closes the SVG Path by drawing a line from last to first point
closepath	Z	Relative	None	Closes the SVG Path by drawing a line from last to first point
lineto	L	Absolute	X, Y	Draws a Line from the current point to the next point
lineto	L	Relative	X, Y	Draws a Line from the current point to the next point
horizontal lineto	H	Absolute	X	Draws a Horizontal Line from current point to next point
horizontal lineto	H	Relative	X	Draws a Horizontal Line from current point to next point
vertical lineto	V	Absolute	Y	Draws a Vertical Line from current point to next point
vertical lineto	V	Relative	Y	Draws a Vertical Line from current point to next point
curveto	C	Absolute	X,Y, X,Y, X,Y	Draws a cubic Bezier curve from current point to next point
curveto	C	Relative	X,Y, X,Y, X,Y	Draws a cubic Bezier curve from current point to next point
Short and smooth curve	S	Absolute	X,Y, X,Y	Draws a cubic Bezier curve from current point to next point
Short and smooth curve	S	Relative	X,Y, X,Y	Draws a cubic Bezier curve from current point to next point
quadratic Bezier curve	Q	Absolute	X,Y, X,Y	Draws a quadratic Bezier curve (current point to next point)
quadratic Bezier curve	Q	Relative	X,Y, X,Y	Draws a quadratic Bezier curve (current point to next point)

(continued)

Table 8-1. *(continued)*

SVG Command	Symbol	Type	Parameter	Description
short quadratic Bezier	T	Absolute	X,Y	Draws a short quadratic Bezier (current point to next point)
short quadratic Bezier	T	Relative	X,Y	Draws a short quadratic Bezier (current point to next point)
elliptical arc	A	Absolute	rX, rY, Rot	Draws an elliptical arc from current point to next
elliptical arc	A	Relative	rX, rY, Rot	Draws an elliptical arc from current point to next

Compound paths are also possible in SVG; these allow you to create complex, Boolean-shaped special effects. For instance, you could use a compound path to create a hole in your shape.

Lines: The Simplest of the Path Components

The simplest way to connect point coordinates along a path is to use straight lines. Different shapes such as triangles, squares, pentagons, and hexagons can be created using the **lineto** commands. There are three lineto commands: a lineto, a horizontal lineto, and a vertical lineto, as outlined in Table 8-1.

To code an octagon using SVG, you use a **moveto** (M) command from a point (vertex) at 60,0 and then draw seven lines using a lineto (L) command. This looks like the following:

```
M 60 0 L 120 0 L 180 60 L 180 120 L 120 180 L 60 180 L 0 120 L 0 60
```

Next let's take a look at the elliptical arc, which is a simple curve by nature with a complex set of specification data for its SVG command, which is why I usually stick with curves, from a modeling perspective, as you will see in Chapter 9.

Elliptical Arcs: Circular and Elliptical Arcs

The last of the three types of curve commands is the elliptical arc, which uses a capital *A* (absolute arc) or a lowercase *a* (relative arc). The arc command draws a segment of an ellipse. It takes the largest number of parameters of any of these curve drawing–related commands and uses the following basic format:

```
M x,y A rx,ry x-axis-rotation large-arc-flag sweep-flag x,y
```

Here, M (moveto) x,y is the starting point of the arc; rx is the **x-radius** for the ellipse; ry is the **y-radius** for the ellipse; x-axis-rotation is the number of degrees to rotate the x-axis, two on/off flags for a large/small arc, and a sweep/no-sweep arc; and the final x,y coordinate is the end point of the arc.

It is important to note that setting both an x and a y radius (the rx and ry values) as identical values creates a circle instead of an ellipse, because this makes the curvature **symmetrical**.

The elliptical arc has a number of parameters, including a coordinate pair, the size of the ellipse being described, an angle, and two flags that alter the rendering. This example also allows you to modify whether the arc coordinates are absolute (A) or relative (a), to the starting point (defined by the red blob). An example of the elliptical arc command and coordinate sequence is shown in Figure 8-1. If you want the missing segment for this ellipse at the bottom, deselect (or set to zero) the large arc flag and the sweep flag, which draws the smaller part of the arc and mirrors it around an x axis. The command for this looks like the following:

```
M 125,300 A 225,100 0 1 1 375,300
```

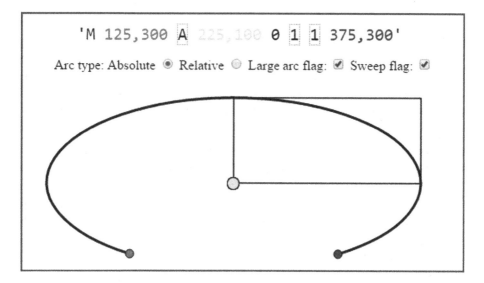

Figure 8-1. *Elliptical arc with Sweep and Large Arc Flags on*

As you can see, the rx,ry parameters create different angles, which distort the shape from being a circle, making it instead elliptical. There are numerous SVG curve generators on the Internet if you want to experiment with these parameters.

Cubic Bezier Curve

If you have ever used the Pen tool in Photoshop or GIMP, or used Inkscape as you will in Chapter 9, or any of the 3D modeling tools out there, then you are probably familiar with **Bézier curves**. I am not going to go into all the math behind how curves are constructed mathematically, as this is a fundamentals book and not an advanced book, but you will look at how to use open source tools to generate the digital illustration vector assets that you need for your Android Studio applications. In a nutshell, you draw **cubic Bézier curves** using SVG commands by defining your start and end points, as well as two control points: one control point for the start point and one control point for the end point. These control the curvature of a curve, also called a **spline** in the industry, going away from the first point and coming into a second point.

The cubic Bézier curve command utilizes this format:

```
M x,y C (or c) x1,y1 x2,y2 x,y
```

The starting point is defined by moveto M x,y, and the C (or c) defines an absolute or relative cubic Bézier curve type. The x1,y1 is your control point for the beginning of the curve, and the x2,y2 is your control point for the end of the curve. Finally, your x,y coordinate at the end of the command string is an end point for the cubic Bézier curve. You will look at how to create Bézier curves in real time with Inkscape in the next chapter.

Quadratic Bezier Curve

There is the inclination to assume that quadratic Bézier curves are more complicated, given that "quad" means four, and therefore that there are even more control points for this type of curve. However, the exact opposite of this is actually the case, because a quadratic Bézier curve actually has only one control point that connects to both the start and the end points of the curve segment, and moving it controls how the curve is shaped between the two points. So if you are looking for coordinate data reduction of 100% as far as control point specification goes, use quadratic Bézier curves. Thus, an SVG command specification for a quadratic Bézier curve looks like the following:

```
M x,y Q (or q) x1,y1 x,y
```

So the quadratic Bézier command requires only one single control point, which is then used as the control point for both the start and end points. So, it's like the two control points in a cubic Bézier curve are connected as one control point, which moves the curvature from the start point and into the end point at the same time. There are numerous SVG curve generators on the Internet, if you want to experiment with the parameters.

The Fill: Filling Your Closed Shapes with Colors

Once you have defined your shape using lines, arcs, and curves, you can fill it to make it solid rather than hollow or empty. A **fill** can be a color, a gradient, or a tiling image pattern. You can fill an open shape if you like, and the (imaginary) line connecting the start point to the end point defines the fill boundary, so the fill does not go all over the place in your digital illustration! The fill operation and the stroke operation, which is covered next, are known as **painting** operations. This is defined in Android Studio using the Paint and Canvas classes.

Color Fill: Filling Your Shape with a Solid Color Value

To fill the octagon you looked at earlier in the line section, a `fill="green"` statement would be added after the data statement, which creates the shape that is filled with a green color. Using SVG XML, these two declarations would be inside of a path XML tag, using the following XML mark-up SVG data structure:

```
<path>
d = "M 60 0 L 120 0 L 180 60 L 180 120 L 120 180 L 60 180 L 0 120 L 0 60"
fill = "green"
</path>
```

Solid fill color is not as useful as gradients, however, as careful use of gradients can even simulate a 3D result using 2D SVG graphics. Defining a gradient is more complex, so, let's take a look at linear and circular gradients next.

Gradient Fills: Linear Gradients and Radial Gradients

There are two types of gradients in SVG, a **linear gradient** and a **radial gradient**. A linear gradient is the most common type of gradient that you will encounter, so let's start with that type first. Much of what applies to how a linear gradient is set up also applies to the radial gradient, which simply uses a different XML tag. I will show you how to set up a `<linearGradient>` tag using SVG in XML and you can simply change it later to be a `<radialGradient>` to change your gradient type.

Gradients are defined in the `<defs>` or "definitions" tag in SVG XML. The `<defs>` tag goes inside the "parent" `<svg>` tag, and has the `<linearGradient>` tag as its "child" tag. Inside the `<linearGradient>` tag are two `<stop>` child tags. **Stops** are used to define the colors in the gradient, the percentage that they make up in the overall gradient, and the alpha or transparency value for that section of the gradient. There must be at least two stops. You can use any amount of gradient sections that you need.

Make sure that your stop offset values add up to **100%** in the end. Here is how you would fill your octagon with red and yellow linear gradients; as you can see, it's much more complex:

```
<svg xmlns='http://www.w3.org/2000/svg' height="300" width="300">
  <defs>
    <linearGradient id="LinearGradient" x1="0%" y1="0%" x2="100%" y2="0%">
      <stop offset="0%" style="stop-color:rgb(255,255,0);stop-opacity:1" />
      <stop offset="100%" style="stop-color:rgb(255,0,0);stop-opacity:1" />
    </linearGradient>
  </defs>
  <path>
    d="M 60 0 L 120 0 L 180 60 L 180 120 L 120 180 L 60 180 L 0 120 L 0 60"
    fill="url(#LinearGradient)"
  </path>
</svg>
```

You wire the gradient into your fill using the id="name" parameter inside of the <linearGradient> tag, and then reference that name inside of your fill="url(#name)" parameter inside of your <path> tag.

Pattern Fill: Filling Your Shape with a Tileable Image Pattern

Patterns are also defined in the <defs> tag in SVG XML. The <pattern> tag goes inside the parent <defs> tag, and has the <image> tag as a child tag. Inside the <image> tag is a reference to and specifications for the image asset. **Patterns** are seamless image tiles that fill a shape with a 2D texture map. You will be learning more about texture maps in Chapter 10.

Make sure that your pattern width and height values match up with your image width and height values. The image X and Y are positioning the start of the pattern at the upper-left corner, which is always location 0,0. Here is how you would fill an octagon with an 8-pixel tiling image pattern; as you will see, it's an even more complex definition than your gradient:

```
<svg xmlns='http://www.w3.org/2000/svg' height="300" width="300">
  <defs>
    <pattern id="pName" patternUnits="userSpaceOnUse" width="8" height="8">
      <image xlink:href="data:image/filename.png"
             x="0" y="0" width="8" height="8">
      </image>
    </pattern>
  </defs>
  <path>
    d="M 60 0 L 120 0 L 180 60 L 180 120 L 120 180 L 60 180 L 0 120 L 0 60"
    fill="url(#pName)"
  </path>
</svg>
```

Although I am showing you how to do this because the book is for Android Studio programmers or developers, most of us use software packages such as Inkscape or Illustrator to create vector artwork and export it to SVG format.

At the end of the work day, however, you'll need to know how to bridge the SVG command structure with your Java code. I will cover the basic SVG commands in this chapter so that you have knowledge of these SVG basics for Android Studio application development.

The Stroke: Controlling How Lines and Curves Look

Finally, let's take a look at how to **stroke** (or color) and **style** (or thicken) the lines, arcs, and curves that you create using these SVG commands. The stroke parameters allow you to define stroke color, opacity, width in pixels, dash array pattern, and how lines will be capped or joined together, using round, square, or bevel constants. Let's add these stroke -related parameters to the <path> that you created earlier for the octagon and give it a 3-pixels-thick black border with rounded corners, a dashed line, and a 50% opacity, using the following SVG XML markup:

```
<path>
d = "M 60 0 L 120 0 L 180 60 L 180 120 L 120 180 L 60 180 L 0 120 L 0 60"
fill = "green"
stroke = "black" stroke-width = "3" stroke-dasharray = "5, 10, 5"
stroke-linecap = "square" stroke-linejoin = "round" stroke-opacity = "0.5"
</path>
```

Next, let's finish up by looking at the primary SVG data commands that you will use in your Android Studio coding, as well as in your CSS3 and JavaFX programming.

SVG Format: Coding Vector Shape Data

There are ten different letters that can be utilized with the numeric (X,Y data point coordinate location) data in SVG data strings. Each has an uppercase (absolute reference) and a lowercase (relative reference) version. As you can see in Table 8-1, SVG data commands provide a great deal of flexibility for defining custom curves in your Android Studio applications development. You can even combine all of these SVG commands with your Java code to create interactive vector (digital illustration) artwork that has never been experienced. Since this is an Android Studio new media fundamentals title, you're going to focus on the new media asset creation process for the majority of the book rather than on an application coding focus, like most of the other books out there.

An optimal way to see how to use these powerful SVG data path drawing commands is to learn a work process for creating SVG data with vector illustration tools and export work flows. You will learn how to do this with Inkscape, using the "quick and dirty" approach; that is, let Inkscape do 90% of the path creation work, and then cut and paste the command data strings into your Java code.

If you're a game programmer, you can also use these path data constructs as collision detection polygons and for similar non-graphical uses of vector data relating to boundaries rather than visual 2D-rendered digital illustration artwork. If you're interested, I cover a workflow to do this using JavaFX's SVGPath class in *Beginning Java 8 Games Development* (Apress, 2015).

Summary

In this chapter, you took a look at digital illustration, also known as **2D vector illustration**, and its related concepts, principles, and SVG formats that are supported in Android Studio, as well as JavaFX and HTML5, using CSS3 and JavaScript. You looked at how vertices or point coordinates, lines, arcs, curves, fills, patterns, gradients, and path stroking can contribute to the digital illustration asset creation process.

In the next chapter, you'll learn **digital Illustration asset creation and data footprint optimization** using Inkscape.

■ ■ ■

CHAPTER 9

Digital Illustration: Data Footprint Optimization

Now that you have an understanding of the fundamental concepts, terminology, and principles regarding digital illustration, it's time to get into how to create 2D vector new media, as well as how to optimize a data footprint.

The real optimization of 2D or 3D vector assets is using it, since raster imagery is inherently data-heavy due to storing large arrays of individual pixel elements in digital images, and individual frames in digital video.

In this chapter, you'll look at how digital illustration is created using the popular open source Inkscape software, so you don't have to write SVG commands and coordinate data by hand with XML markup or Java code. You'll also learn how to export these commands and coordinate data strings using a work process that has Inkscape write your SVG vector object's data as XML or Java code for you.

Inkscape: Vector Illustration Shape Data

Since vector new media assets are inherently optimized, as long as you use the smallest number of vertices possible to create 2D and 3D assets, and the correct types of Bezier splines for your objective, you can focus on how to use Inkscape to create 2D vector assets. In this chapter, you'll also learn how to use Export functions to turn these into command data and XML markup that you can use in Android Studio, and in JavaFX and HTML5 as well.

With vector images this is accomplished with coordinates in the 2D X,Y space, along with mathematics that define curves conveyed using SVG instructions, which look a lot like code. Let's cover the basic constructs of vector illustration.

The Layout: Overview of Key Areas in Inkscape

The Inkscape user interface is quite complex, as this software gives you virtually everything you need for your 2D vector new media asset creation workflow. In a nutshell, there are three vertical toolbars: the **primary function** tools on the left, the **snap settings** on the far right, and the **command tools** on the inside right toolbar (see Figure 9-1).

© Wallace Jackson 2015
W. Jackson, *Android Studio New Media Fundamentals*,
DOI 10.1007/978-1-4842-9867-1_9

There is also the **floating palette docking** area on the right side of the **canvas**, which is the white area that occupies the majority of your UI. At the very top are menus, and underneath that is a horizontal toolbar containing options for the selected tool; in Figure 9-1 this is the **Edit paths by nodes** tool, as a pop-up tooltip shows on the left. (I'm featuring it in this screenshot because it is a tool you'll use to create complex spline data for your Android Studio games and applications.) At the bottom of the UI is a **color swatch selector** for shape fills and curve stroking, and underneath that is a **status bar** for numeric representation of what you are doing and other important workflow settings. The square in the middle of your UI is the **page** you are working on.

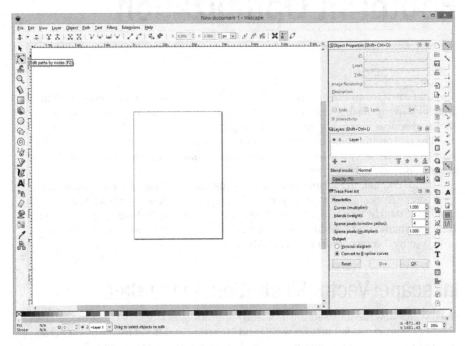

Figure 9-1. *Inkscape tools, floating palettes, option selectors*

Let's get right to learning how to use shape creation tools in Inkscape and how to export the XML path command data.

Polygon Shapes: Creating Basic Closed Shapes

Polygon shapes, which are covered further in Chapter 10, are shapes that have straight lines on their perimeter, like triangles, squares, pentagons, hexagons, and octagons. Let's use the Inkscape polygon tool to create the green octagon you created with SVG commands in Chapter 9. Select the **Create stars and polygons** tool shown in Figure 9-2. Then select the polygon option on the top left of the options toolbar. Set your **Corners** spinner to **8**, and then click the middle of the page and pull out the octagon. You can use the **Fill and Stroke** color palette, seen on the top right, to set the fill color to green.

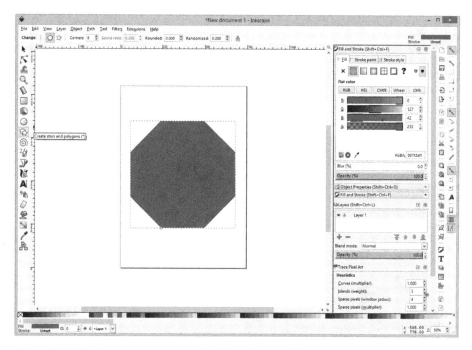

Figure 9-2. *Create a green octagon using the polygon tool*

You can control the size and the rotation of this polygon when you pull it out from the center. I made the sizes align with the top, bottom, and sides of the page.

As you can see at the bottom left, the stroke and fill attributes are summarized, as is the layer that you are drawing the shape on. The Opacity of 100% is shown in gray in a palette on the right side of the screen, for both the fill and Layer 1, as you'll see in the SVG path data you're about to export. Let's take a look at how to turn this shape into SVG path data next.

SVG Data Export: Using Inkscape File ➤ Save As

Many open source packages, such as GIMP and Blender, use a **File ➤ Save as** menu sequence to save their native file format, and use a File ➤ Export menu sequence to save different data formats. Inkscape uses File ➤ Save As to save (export) into different data formats, as shown in Figure 9-3. Use **Plain SVG** to get XML data that you can edit and extract your Path command data from.

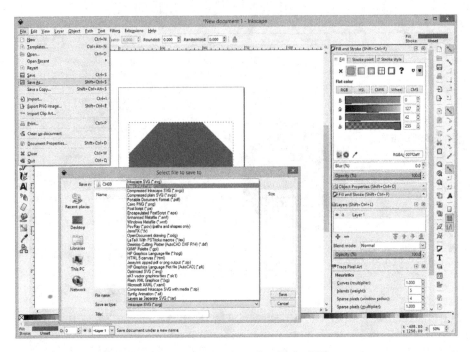

Figure 9-3. *Use File ➤ Save As menu sequence; select Plain SVG*

Name the file **octagon.svg** and open it in a text editor, as shown in Figure 9-4. Your Path data string is shown in blue.

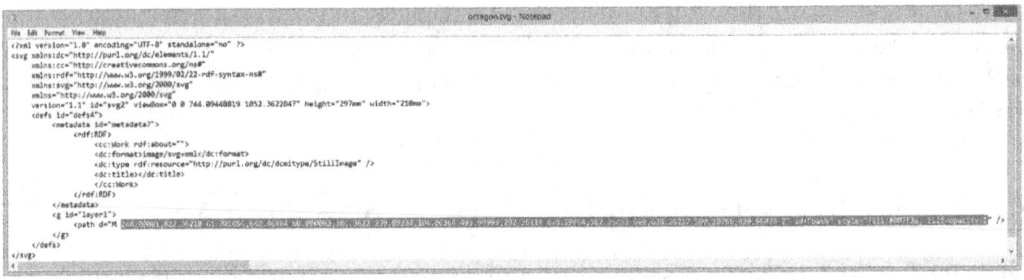

Figure 9-4. *Open this octagon.svg file in your OS text editor*

You may have noticed the JavaFX and HTML5 export support, as well as other platforms, such as PostScript and Flash, in the Save As dialog in Figure 9-3. If you are going to use JavaFX in Android or iOS, you use this option, but using plain SVG is the best way to extract the raw SVG command data string for the path that you are creating in Inkscape. If you have a complex, multi-layer construct, there is also the **Layers as Separate SVG** option, so you can keep your SVG path command data modularized.

Spline Shapes: Creating Complex Shapes

I'll let you play around with the other basic shape tools, like the elliptical arc tool and the text tool. In this chapter, the focus is on drawing polygons and Bezier splines. These topics are also covered in the next chapter, which focuses on 3D new media, so I'll get you used to them in a 2D vector software package. Besides, most of what you create for your Android Studio applications will be made out of polygons or Bezier splines, so it is practical to focus on these shape creation tools in Inkscape.

Using the Draw Bezier Curves Tool: Drawing Your Rough Shape

Start a New Project in Inkscape with a **File ➤ New** menu sequence. Select **the Draw Bezier curves and straight lines** tool. This is seen on the left side of the screen in Figure 9-5, about halfway down the Inkscape toolbar. I left the tooltip visible so that you could see it more easily. You can mouse-over tools and other user interface elements to see what they do simply by using this handy pop-up tooltip functionality. Now, let's create a complex Bezier spline shape, such as a heart, and only use four data points to do it (since this chapter is about optimization). As I mentioned, the way to optimize a vector is to use fewer data points and leverage spline tensioning handles.

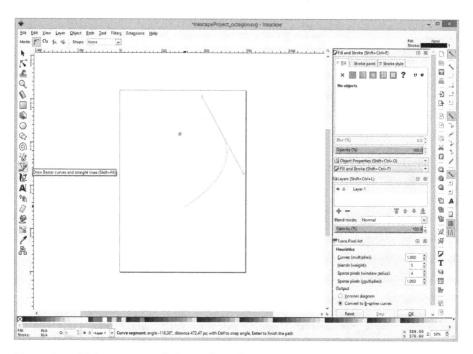

Figure 9-5. *Click start point, click to right, pull out handles*

To create a heart in Inkscape, select the **Draw Bezier curves and straight lines** tool, and click in the center of your page about 25% down from the top. The starting point in Inkscape is shown by using a hollow square point.

Click a second point to the right of this starting point, close to the page's right side. In Figure 9-5, this is shown where blue spline tensioning handles meet and the green curve segment (one) and red current curve segment (two) meet.

Pull out the spline handles from the second point as you click (and drag) it to create the rough curve. You'll fine-tune this later on, so it does not have to be perfect. Once you let go (released the mouse-down to stop the drag handles mode), you can move the spline down, toward the bottom of the heart.

Next, click the point that will be the bottom point for the heart shape, which should be directly underneath the start point and about 60% down from the top of the page, or 40% up from the bottom of the page.

Draw your third segment of the heart curve up to a point that is the opposite, or mirror image of, the second point, on the left side of your starting point this time. This should be about the same distance from the left edge of the page as your second point was from the right side of your page, as shown in Figure 9-6. Click your third point to the left of the starting point, close to the page's left side. This is shown where blue spline tensioning handles meet, and where the green curve segment (three) and red current curve segment (four) meet, as seen in Figure 9-6.

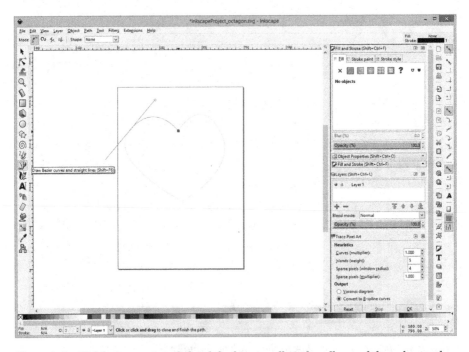

Figure 9-6. *Click bottom point, click to left of start, pull out handles, and then place end point of heart over start point*

Again, pull out your spline handles from the third point as you click and drag it to create a rough curve. Once you have let go (released the mouse-down to stop the drag handles mode), you can move the fourth curve segment end point, this time over the starting point of your heart shape (path). If you position the end point of a path draw operation over your starting point for the path draw operation, the mutual point will turn red, as seen in Figure 9-6. You can then click to close the heart's path.

Once you click the start point, the fifth end point and the start point become the same (start) point, so you have used only four points and only four curve segments to create an optimized closed heart shape (path).

Once you close the shape, the green and red segment color guides disappear, and your entire Bezier spline curve is colored black and is one pixel in thickness. Note that this simply shows you where your Bezier curve path is, because a path actually has no thickness, mathematically speaking.

As you can see in Figure 9-7, the left side of the heart actually came out better than the right side did. In this next section of the chapter, you will look at how to edit spline curve constructs in Inkscape.

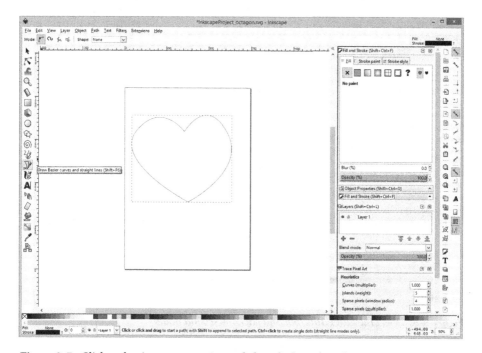

Figure 9-7. *Click end point on start point and close the heart's path*

Editing a path is done with a different Inkscape tool, called the **Edit paths by nodes** tool. It is provided so that an artist can go back and fine-tune node (control point or vertex) handles, or so vector artists can further edit existing paths.

Notice that there are many different terms used for the points (control points), or vertices, or nodes, or coordinates, which make up a path (shape) comprised of Bezier spline curves.

Next, let's refine the heart and improve its path shape using the **Edit paths by nodes** tool, one of the most often-used tools in Inkscape, as indicated by its location right underneath the Arrow (Selection) tool in the Inkscape primary toolbar.

Using the Edit Paths by Nodes Tool: Refining Your Heart Shape

The icon for the Edit Path tool (for short) shows an acute triangle cursor selecting a node for editing, with spline tensioning handles telescoping out of the node. Once you select this tool, your heart shape shows the nodes (points, or vertices), which are between Bezier curve segments, as hollow points. This tool is shown selected (in blue) in Figure 9-8.

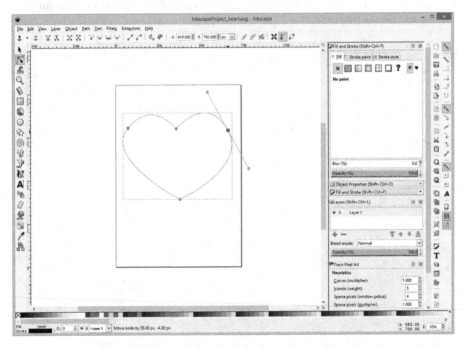

Figure 9-8. *Select the Edit Paths tool and click the second node*

Let's start by selecting the second node, located on the right side of the heart. Once you click and select this node, it turns red and spline tensioning handles emerge from the node. These control curvature for two different curve segments on each side of the node. The top handle, moved using the circle at the end of the handle, controls the curvature of where line segment one is coming into vertex number two.

The bottom handle, which is also moved with the circle at the end of the handle, controls the curvature of where line segment two is coming out of vertex two.

Moving the spline handle's end point changes the angle of the handle and affects the curvature of your curve, which is attached to the vertex and defined with that vertex, as you learned in Chapter 8.

If you shorten or lengthen the handles by moving the end points closer to (or farther from) the vertex itself, the curve becomes more curved by using longer handles, or less curved by using shorter spline tensioning handles.

If you put your handle points on top of, or retract them back into, the vertex, it then becomes a corner point, and the curve coming out of the point becomes a line (polygon).

There are also different keyboard modifiers that turn on angle snap (Control), lock your curvature (Alternate), or handle length, and break the handle symmetry coming out of the vertex or node (Shift). This is a tool that you will need to practice using for a length of time to become proficient or professional in its usage. Be sure to explore the Edit Paths by Node Tool option toolbar at the top-left of Inkscape, as well.

The first thing you need to fix in this currently imperfect heart path is the bulbous right side. To fix this curvature, you need to adjust the curve coming out of your second vertex, which is done by using the lower segment of the tensioning handle, shown (along with the heart defect) in Figure 9-8; it is shown selected in red (fixed) in Figure 9-9.

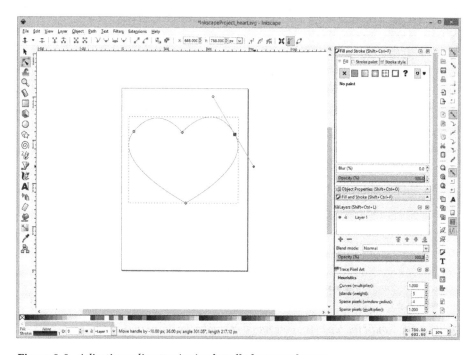

Figure 9-9. *Adjusting spline tensioning handle for second curve*

If you want to follow along with the heart surgery you're doing in Inkscape, you can open your InkscapeProject_heart.svg file in the repository for this book.

To reduce the ballooning of the curve on the right side of the heart, pull the end point of the lower handle closer, until the second curve becomes symmetrical to the third curve, as shown in Figure 9-9.

As you can see if you compare Figure 9-8 and Figure 9-9, I have shortened the handle length about 15%, reducing the amount of curve as well.

Using the **Edit paths by nodes** tool requires what's often called "tweaking," which means making slight adjustments to the vertices and their tensioning handles more than one time around so as to gradually refine a shape, in this case, it is a heart.

Now that the bottom part (curve) of vertex two is adjusted, let's work on the top part; that is, the curve coming into vertex two.

As you can see in Figure 9-9, the top-right half of the heart is square-ish and needs to be more rounded like the left half.

As you can see in Figure 9-10, I have shortened the top part of the spline tensioning handle by about 15% to make the curvature match the other (left) side of the heart shape better again by reducing an amount of curvature coming into the second vertex.

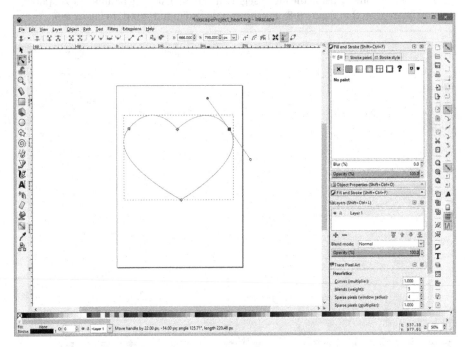

Figure 9-10. *Adjust the top tensioning handle to make the shape rounder*

Now the top half of the heart is improved, and you should now start to tweak the center points on the top and the bottom to continue to refine this heart shape even more.

Pull down the bottom vertex to refine the height of the heart, as shown in Figure 9-11. Since the tip of the heart does not have any round curves (it is sharp), this means that spline tensioning handles are directly on top of the third vertex.

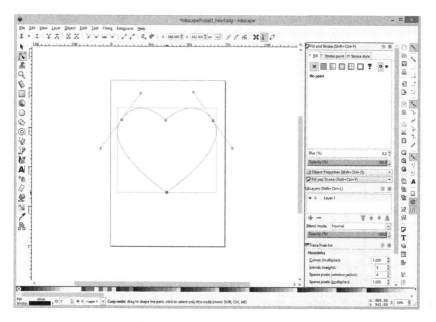

Figure 9-11. *Pull down the bottom vertex and center it with top*

If you want to stylize the bottom of the heart, hold down the Shift key and pull out the spline tensioning handle of the vertex. I show this in Figure 9-13 so that you can see what I mean.

You can pull down the top point, as seen in Figure 9-12.

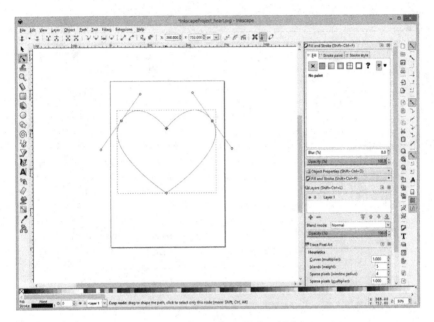

***Figure 9-12.** Pull down the top vertex and center it with bottom*

At this point in the tweaking process, the heart's shape is just a matter of taste, so continue to tweak the four Bezier curve vertices until you have the result that you desire.

If you want to stylize the tip of the heart, located at vertex three, you can drag the tensioning handles back out of the sharp corner, as is seen in Figure 9-13, by holding down the **Shift** keyboard modifier, clicking the selected vertex, and dragging your mouse away from the selected (red) control point (node or vertex).

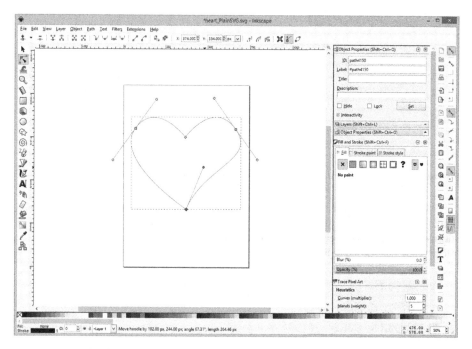

Figure 9-13. *Use the Shift key and drag handle out of vertex #3*

Since this is a data footprint optimization chapter, I will show you how to trim 47 characters (about half) of the SVG command string data from your heart path vector definition.

Data Footprint Optimization: Use Integers

Use the **File ➤ Save As ➤ Plain SVG** work process that you learned in the first part of this chapter and name the file **heart_PlainSVG** (as is shown at the top (title bar) of the screen in Figure 9-14). Format your data (I did it for you here) using the indented XML convention, and take a look at the command data, which is in the quotes after the d= inside of the child <path> tag.

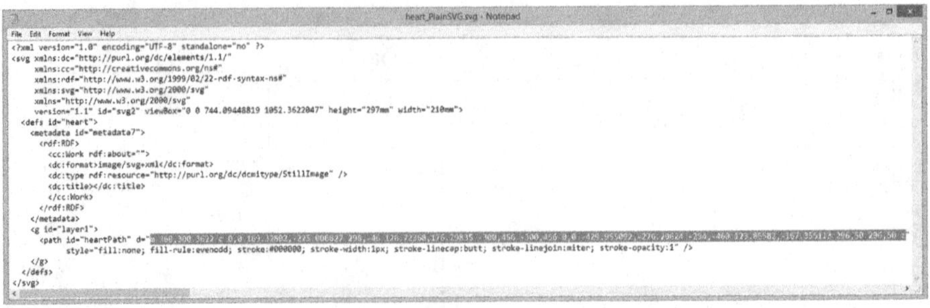

Figure 9-14. *View the floating point version of your path data*

As you see, the coordinate data has extremely precise floating-point accuracy, which is not necessarily accuracy in an Android Studio application writing to a screen that addresses pixels using integer values. Round these floating-point values to the nearest integer value, as shown in Figure 9-15.

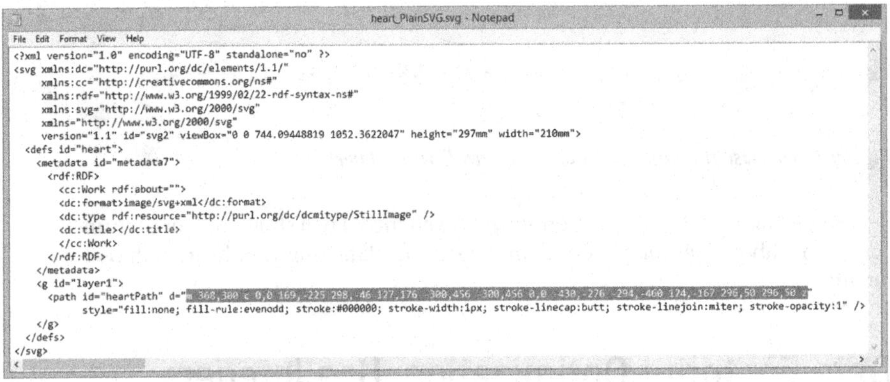

Figure 9-15. *Convert your floating-point data into integer data*

This reduces the vector data footprint by about 100%.

Summary

In this chapter, you looked at digital illustration data footprint optimization as well as how to use the Inkscape vector illustration software. You saw how to create spline and polygon shapes, as well as how to export the SVG command data and how to optimize if for use in Android Studio and Java.

In the next chapter, you will learn **3D asset creation and data footprint optimization** using Blender.

CHAPTER 10

3D New Media: Concepts and Terminology

Now that you have an understanding of the fundamental concepts, terminology, principles, and data footprint optimization for your 2D digital image, digital audio, digital video, and vector digital illustration new media content for Android Studio, it's time to get into the more complicated area of 3D new media assets, which in Android Studio can become i3D, or interactive 3D, assets for game applications, e-learning, and simulations.

Android Studio only supports one open source, real-time, i3D vector rendering platform, called **OpenGL**, which stands for **Open Graphics Library**. Unlike SVG, which is relatively simple in comparison with OpenGL, I cannot cover i3D in just a couple of chapters, or even within a couple of books for that matter.

If you are creating i3D OpenGL apps with Android Studio, however, this is entirely a different type of app. If you want to develop 3D apps for Android, you need to get books dedicated to and specializing in that specifically, as 3D is a whole different ballgame compared to other new media asset support found in Android Studio and the Android OS. Like those new media assets that are supported in Android, Android i3D support is entirely open source, so that is certainly good news.

In this chapter, I'll give you as much of an overview of 3D as I can, as it is far more expansive than your 2D new media assets, and not just because it has the third dimension (depth) or fourth dimension (animation) that digital video and digital audio also have. The primary reason is its use to create photo-realistic environments out of thin air, which has been primarily driven by the console game industry as well as by the Hollywood film industry. You can take advantage of these 3D advancements!

You'll look at the basic concepts, principles, and formats used in 3D vector images, 3D animation, 3D modeling, 3D texture mapping, 3D particle effects, 3D physics simulations, character animation, and all the similarly complex i3D-related topics.

Interactive 3D Assets: 3D Vector Content

Interactive 3D vector objects can be created with Android code, using Java 7 or JavaFX classes and methods, or with 3D software packages, such as Autodesk 3D Studio Max (which is what I use), or Blender, an open source software nearing a similar level of professional features.

© Wallace Jackson 2015
W. Jackson, *Android Studio New Media Fundamentals*,
DOI 10.1007/978-1-4842-9867-1_10

Interactive 3D, commonly known as i3D, vector assets are primarily comprised of 3D vector geometry, or vertices, in a 3D space. This is surfaced with 2D raster images, which you learned about in Chapter 2, and animated using keyframes, which you saw used in Chapter 6. To make 3D interactive, you define your 3D object (internal) **hierarchy**, and imbed **programming logic** for each part of the 3D object that tells it how to function. There are a lot more "layers" to creating a static 3D or dynamic i3D object than you find in the 2D new media areas of Android Studio.

It is important to note that all of your other new media assets are incorporated in i3D new media assets. This means everything you learned about in the first nine chapters are a part of a complex i3D model creation work process as well, as you will soon see. Digital imagery is used to skin 3D model geometry, digital video provides animated texture maps, SVG geometry is used or rendered onto 3D surfaces for texture mapping effects, and digital audio is used for sound effects or to make i3D characters speak. The possibilities are endless.

Let's start from the vertex on up, like you did in the 2D vector illustration chapter. I will show you various attributes that take a 3D asset from being **3D geometry** to being a **3D model** to being a **3D hierarchy** to being a **3D animation** to being an **i3D object**.

The vertex is the least commonly used new media asset type; it is found in HTML5 (web sites and smartphones) by using WebGL 2, in Android by using OpenGL ES 3.1, and in Java 7, 8, and 9 by using JavaFX.

The Foundation of 3D: The Geometry of the Mesh

Just as with 2D SVG new media, the lowest level of 3D new media assets is the vertex and its connection with other vertices. With 3D, connections between vertices become more complicated, not only because these occur in three dimensions, but also because 3D introduces triangular faces commonly called **polygons** or "polys," or rectangular faces, called **quadrilaterals**, or "quads." The connections between vertices are called "edges." Before 3D geometry is texture mapped, it's referred to in the 3D industry as a "mesh," or a "wireframe," since that is what your 3D geometry looks like before it is **texture mapped** or "skinned" using digital imagery. You will cover this in the next section.

Data Points in a 3D Space: Origins of the 3D Vertex

Just like the 2D vertices (or "anchor points" as they're called in Illustrator, or "path nodes" as they are called using Inkscape) the vertex is the foundation of 3D geometric and organic modeling. Just as 2D polygons use straight lines, 3D geometric models use straight lines, and 3D organic models use 3D curves defined with NURBS (non-uniform rational B-spline), Catmull-Rom splines, and Hash patches. The vertex defines where your model's infrastructure—whether it is edges or splines—is located in 3D space.

In 3D geometry, vertex data can hold **surface color** data, **surface normals** data, **UVW texture mapping** data, as well as the vertex **X, Y, Z location** data. This is similar to pixels in 2D, which hold X and Y data; RGB data; and alpha channel data.

Those of you who are familiar with 3D data scanners know the term "point clouds." So vertices are still the foundation for everything that you create in the 3D industry, from games to simulations to virtual worlds and beyond.

For Java 7, 8, and 9 programming, the JavaFX **VertexFormat** class holds vertex data that includes vertex location, normal information (normal are covered soon), and 3D texture coordinates. So you can place the vertices for your game or IoT application with JavaFX code, or you can use a 3D modeler such as Hexagon, or a 3D modeler and animation package like Blender.

Connect the 3D Vertices: Edges Bridge 3D Vertices Together

3D geometric models use something called an **edge** to connect two vertices together. An edge is a **vector**, or straight line, so it looks like the edge of a razor in 3D space, as you can see in Blender in Figure 10-1. Three edges are needed to form polygons, and four edges are needed to form quads. Polygons and quads are called "faces," which are covered in the next section. When you're modeling 3D geometric objects, you can select components of a model, such as a vertex, an edge, or a polygon.

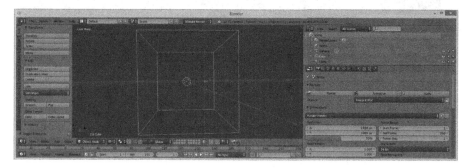

Figure 10-1. *Blender 3D geometry having 8 vertices and 12 edges*

If you've created 3D geometry using a more advanced spline-based modeling paradigm, such as NURBS using MoI 3D, or quads using SILO 2 (only $160), or Hash patches using Animation:Master (only $80), you'll need to "decimate" your model into polygons (triangles), which is what Android Studio (OpenGL, Java, JavaFX) uses for its 3D rendering.

Currently, there is no OpenGL "native" rendering support for splines or quads in Android, JavaFX, or HTML5. All of these use OpenGL ES 3.1. The ES stands for "Embedded Systems," and refers to portable, low-power consumer electronics devices.

The algorithmic process of **decimation** from other spline or quadrilateral representations of 3D geometry into polygons turns the infinitely smooth curves used in these modeling paradigms into a collection of triangular faces with straight edges.

This is done by using a decimation or **smoothness** numeric factor, via a slider or dialog setting. This is either the decimation function inside of the 3D software or it is supplied in a File Export function that outputs the spline modeling format from a curve-based modeler into a polygonal geometric model format. A great example of this is in the Moment of Inspiration V3 NURBS modeling software. Now let's take a look at how polygons, quads, and splines form 3D **surfaces**.

Surface: Three Edges Form a Polygon, Four Edges Form a Quad

Once you have three edges together in the format of a triangle, you have a polygon. This can be used as a **surface** and can host a "skin" or "texture" to make the 3D data look more realistic. The rule of thumb is that the more uniform (square) a triangle is, the better it will render. **Slivered** (long, thin triangles) can cause rendering "artifacts" or visual anomalies, but often do not. You feeling lucky? Then use slivered polygons. Modelers often prefer modeling with quads and keep them as square as possible using quad modelers such as the popular Silo 2.3 from NeverCenter (shown in Figure 10-2), which is only $109.

Figure 10-2. *Silo quad modeling software is affordable at $109*

As you can see, Silo (currently at version 2.3.1) can be used for character modeling. This is usually accomplished using organic spline modelers, such as Hash Animation:Master (seen in Figure 10-3) using a proprietary **Hash patch** spline algorithm.

Figure 10-3. *Hash A:M character modeling software is only $79*

Once you have a surface, which needs to be a triangle for Android, you have also defined your **surface normal**. In the Blender 2.76 project shown in Figure 10-1, the faces on the basic cube are quads, but as you will see, quads, just like tris, have surface normals as well.

Normals are one of the things used to apply the texture map to 3D mesh geometry to make it look solid.

Texture mapping is covered in the next major section of this chapter. There is a principle that is related to **adjacent polygons** or faces that is called a **smoothing group**, which you will take a look at after surface normals.

Therefore, at the very least, a surface polygon, triangle, quad, or face contains data for one normal, several texture maps, and a smoothing group. As I mentioned, i3D assets are significantly more advanced than 2D media assets. 3D assets are rendered on the client side, or on the device that they're being viewed on. I cover rendering later on in the chapter as well. Lots of i3D topics to cover!

The Direction a Surface is Facing: The Concept of Surface Normals

If you know how to turn the "show normals" feature on in the 3D software, you can see your 3D face **surface normals**, which are displayed at the exact center of the face, as you can see in light blue in Figure 10-4. There are also buttons in Blender for showing **vertex normals**, which point outward from a vertex; so for this model, vertex normals point out diagonally from the corners of the cube (45 degrees), the exact opposite result from the face normals, which point straight up (90 degrees, like a skyscraper) from the center of each face.

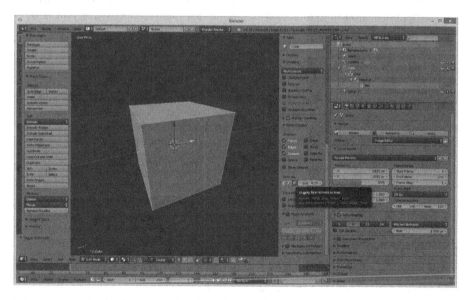

Figure 10-4. Display face normals as lines button shows normals

As you can see in Figure 10-4, two of the normals seen are actually aligned with the X (red) and Y (green) axes, which intersect the cube at 90 degrees. Your axis guide, in the lower-left corner of the 3D Edit Mode view, shows which axis is X, which is Y, and which is Z.

105

The function for this surface normal is fairly simple. A surface normal tells a rendering engine the **direction** a surface is facing: inward or outward. The same logic applies to a vertex normal; it shows the rendering engine which side of the 3D geometry to process for surface rendering.

If your normals for this cube geometry had been pointing inward, instead of outward, this cube would not be visible at all when rendered. There's a **flip normals** operation (algorithm) in 3D software that is used to **reverse** your normal directions. This is done for the model universally; all normals are flipped 180 degrees.

Flip normals are utilized when you render the scene and your imported 3D object is not visible after you render the scene. This is almost always because a 3D import utility points (flips) the surface normals for the imported 3D geometry in the wrong direction. An exporter from a 3D modeling tool might have exported the surface normal in the wrong direction, relative to the software you are importing them in. This is a fairly common occurrence, so, expect to use flip normals regularly if you are going to work with 3D or i3D new media assets.

If you need something—like a house, for instance—in which the 3D geometry has to render from the outside and from the inside (this is common in 3D virtual worlds, which are also inherently i3D simulations), because you have to be able to navigate through them, you have to create your geometry's faces as **double-sided polygons**. You need to apply a double-sided texture map, which I'll cover in the next section.

It is important to note that in i3D, using double-sided geometry and double-sided textures requires significantly more real-time rendering engine processing by your CPU and FPU.

Smoothing a Faceted Surface: Using Smoothing Groups

You have seen 3D models that are rendered as solid (instead of wireframe) but look like they are chiseled; that is, you can see the polygons (faces) rendered as if they were flat, as seen in Figure 10-5. This is often called **flat shaded**; no smoothing is applied by the rendering engine. If you render the same geometry with smoothing turned on, this effect disappears and the 3D geometry looks as it was intended to, which is infinitely smooth, like it was created using splines, when it is actually using polygons. It is more efficient to have the rendering engine do the smoothing than to have a ton of mesh (polygon) data. The renderer applies smoothing using something called **smoothing group**, which is applied to each face to tell the renderer when to smooth between two faces and when not to, which leaves what is commonly referred to as a "seam." A smoothing group uses simple integer numbers. If the numbers match on each side of an edge (for each adjacent face on the opposite side of that edge), it renders as a smooth color transition. If the numbers are different, it renders a seam and the edge is clearly visible because the color gradients on each side of the edge are different, so the color gradient is not seamless across the two faces (polygons).

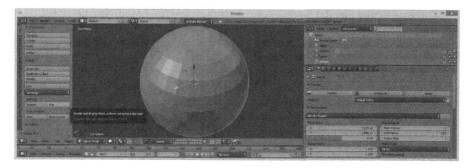

Figure 10-5. *Set faceted shading via Transform ➤ Shading ➤ Flat*

In some 3D software packages, such as Autodesk 3D Studio Max, the smoothing group numbering schema is in the user interface. In others, such as Blender, the numbering is hidden and the smoothing group's function is "exposed" by using the Mark Seam, Clear Seam, Mark Sharp, or Clear Sharp commands in the Blender Edges menu, which is seen on the left of Figure 10-6 with the Mark Sharp option selected in blue.

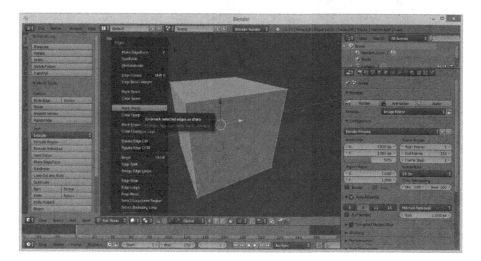

Figure 10-6. *The Blender Edges menu allows you to set smoothing*

In Blender, some 3D modelers (people, not software) make the mistake of trying to expose a seam or a sharp edge in their 3D geometry by actually splitting an edge in 3D geometry itself, which achieves this visual effect but could also cause a problem during the 3D geometry topology refinement work process, as your model is continually refined. Splitting geometry edges to achieve a seam can be avoided by using the Mark Seam or the Mark Sharp edge modifiers in Blender.

These particular Blender modifiers are smoothing groups–based, and therefore achieve a smoothing (or edge seam) effect without actually affecting the 3D geometry topology itself. The 3D geometry **topology** is how the polygons are laid out relative to each other.

A modifier in Blender is applied right before rendering, and therefore doesn't actually affect your actual mathematical topology for your underlying 3D geometry. If you are familiar with the term "topography" used in mapping, then topology is very similar, as it is a 3D term that refers to how the surface of the 3D geometry is constructed.

Using the Blender modifier is always a more flexible i3D content creation approach, as it applies a smoothness or other desired effects or results at the rendering engine level, and not at the 3D geometry topological level. This leaves a 3D mesh intact and ultimately simpler. As always, simpler is better.

You can apply smoothing to a 3D model globally (to all faces at the same time) by using the **Transform** panel and the **Shading** panel area, and then clicking the **Smooth** button, as shown in Figure 10-7. This applies the smoothing group to the entire model, resulting in a smooth surface color gradient.

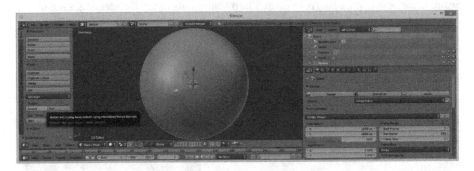

Figure 10-7. *Set smoothing using Transform* ➤ *Shading* ➤ *Smooth*

Next, let's take a look at how to apply a "skin" to your mesh geometry surface, using something called **texture mapping**.

Skinning a 3D Model: Texture Mapping Concepts

Once your 3D geometry is completed, which is the foundation for your 3D model, you can apply texture maps to it to create a solid appearance for your 3D model. Texture maps can also be used to add detail and special effects to a 3D model, making it appear more realistic. If you are wondering what the difference is between 3D geometry and a 3D model, 3D geometry is just the mesh or wireframe, whereas a 3D model should have texture maps already applied. If you purchase third-party 3D models, you expect them to look as they are supposed to when rendered, instead of being flat gray, which is what a rendered model looks like without any texture mapping (and no vertex color) information applied, as seen in Figure 10-7.

Texture Map Basics: Channels, Shading, Effects, and UVW Maps

Texture mapping is almost as complex an area of 3D as creating topologically correct geometry. In fact, each area of 3D is equally complex, which is what makes 3D the most complex new media type overall. This is why 3D feature films employ artists to specifically focus on (work on) and handle each of the areas you are looking at in this chapter. Texture mapping is one of the primary areas in 3D new media asset production that is able to use 2D vector and 2D raster image assets.

It's important to note that there is also a more complex area of 3D texture mapping that uses 3D texture algorithms. It is commonly termed **volumetric texturing**; it uses algorithms to create true 3D texturing effects that go all the way through a 3D object, as though it were a solid, and not a hollow or a 3D object that requires double-sided texture mapping.

A basic concept behind texture mapping is taking the assets that you have learned about in this book, and applying 2D assets to the surface of the 3D geometry. This is accomplished by using UVW mapping coordinates. These 3D coordinates show how you want the 2D image (plane) oriented to or projected on your 3D geometry surface topology. UVW used to be different than XYZ, but they represent the same dimensions (width, height, depth). There's a need to use different letters than XYZ, thus the three letters in the alphabet before XYZ (UVW-XYZ, so that you don't get confused applying your texture mapping coordinates!).

You can add more than one texture map to the surface of your 3D geometry by using **texture channels**. These are analogous to the color and alpha channels that you use in your 2D image to define each pixel's characteristics. Open platforms such as Android, HTML5, and JavaFX currently support four of the most important texture channels. These include the **diffuse** texture map (basic ARGB color values), the **specular** texture map (where surface is shiny or dull), the **illumination** texture map (also called a **glow** map), and the **bump** texture map.

3D software supports other advanced texture map channel types used for additional texturing effects. To bring them into Android, you have to use a process called "texture baking."

Baking texture maps involves rendering all the texture's channels into a primary diffuse texture map, since that is what Android supports. This provides a similar visual result to what you get when you render your 3D object in your 3D package.

As you can see in Figure 10-8, Blender 2.76 also uses a scene graph, just like most modern-day 3D software packages do, and JavaFX offers this same scene graph functionality as well.

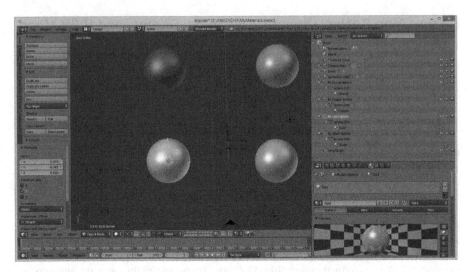

Figure 10-8. *Using a scene graph (right) to apply a gold texture map and shader (bottom) to a sphere object in Blender*

This sphere geometry and its texture mapping are grouped together in a scene graph hierarchy, which I have expanded for you. The texture map definition contains one or more texture channel; in this case, diffuse (color) and specular (surface characteristics such as shininess, metalicity, and the like).

As you can see in Figure 10-8, you can get a lot of good skinning results out of the few texture channels that are now supported in open platforms such as Android, JavaFX, and HTML5.

As time goes on, OpenGL ES 3.1 could add even more texture channel support, giving developers increased visual flexibility for their 3D new media asset usage. Transparency areas (opacity maps) and surface details (normal maps) are two of the most important areas of advanced texture mapping support that needs to be added to Android Studio, JavaFX, and HTML5.

These will ultimately need to be added to Android Studio either by supporting the JavaFX API so that developers are able to create realistic 3D models for Java 7, 8 or 9, or by using **Android Extension Package** (AEP) from nVidia, which you currently have to install, but eventually will become a permanent part of Android Studio, Android APIs, and the Android OS.

A **shader definition** is a collection of texture channels and any code governing these channels' relationship to each other, as well as how they are composited, applied, and rendered relative to each other.

Shaders are also commonly referred to as "materials" in the industry. Shaders and shader languages (another specialized and complex area of 3D and i3D Android Studio applications development) are covered in the next section. As you can see, there are a lot of "layers" to i3D production—and where shaders are concerned, sublayers!

Shader Design: Shader Channels and GLSL Shader Language

As are each of the areas of 3D object creation covered in this chapter, texture map shader design is another art form in and of itself. Hundreds of shader artists work on 3D movies, popular console games, and television shows, ensuring that the shaders used to texture or skin the 3D geometry makes the resulting 3D model look as real as possible. This is often the primary objective of 3D and i3D: to replace more expensive video camera shoots (and subsequent reshoots) by creating a virtual world and having the computers (render farm) create all the camera movements for you, turning them into pixels (imagery), frames (video), or experiences (game or apps).

The basic shader is made up of a series of vector shapes and raster images (or algorithmic, volumetric textures) held in different types of texture channels. These texture channels use the vector and raster assets to apply various types of effects, such as diffusion (RGB color channels), opacity (transparency), glow (self-illumination), specularity (surface characteristics), environmental (surroundings), bump (height), normal (topology), and similar detail effect channels that increase photo-realism.

On top of this, advanced shader languages like the **Open GL Shader Language** (**GLSL**) use code to define how these channels interrelate to each other, how to apply or process the data contained in the channels, and other complex applications of the data within these channels based on factors such as time, orientation, or a position in i3D space. The complex nature of shaders also means that the more complex that a shader becomes, the more time-consuming the render-time processing cycle becomes.

This is probably the primary reason OpenGL ES3 currently supports the four basic easiest-to-process shaders. As hardware becomes more powerful (4- or 8-core CPUs in consumer electronics products), OpenGL ES will probably add the last two important shader channels: opacity (alpha channel) and normals mapping.

Once texture channels are defined inside of the shaders, you need to **orient** the 2D assets to the 3D geometry, which is done by using **texture mapping coordinates**. Each channel has its own coordinate system, if needed, to apply each of the effects to the mesh to achieve the desired effect.

This is accomplished using something called **UVW mapping**, which is also be covered in the next section before you move into the fourth dimension and learn about 3D animation principles and terminology.

Texture Map Orientation: Projection Types and UVW Coordinates

It is important to **align** the detail features in your 2D texture map channels (especially the foundational diffuse color channel as it paints or colors the surface of your object) to your i3D geometry correctly. If you don't do this correctly, some fairly odd, or at least visually incorrect, results appear when the 3D object is rendered. The alignment needs to be done in 3D space, because texture mapping this is UVW (especially with a volumetric "true 3D" texture, but also for 2D textures) to define how they project onto, on top of, or envelop around i3D geometry.

One of the easier ways this is done is by applying a **texture map projection type** and its related settings. This automatically sets your **UVW mapping** numeric values for you. These **UVW map coordinate** values define how your 2D imagery plane maps onto the 3D geometry in 3D space. This provides your "mathematical bridge," between your 2D space and your 3D space. UVW map **floating point** values can be set or tweaked manually to fine-tune the visual result of the texture mapping.

The simplest type of projection is the **planar projection**, because a plane is a simple 2D square. You visualize this type of mapping as if your 2D texture map image were in front of the 3D object, and you were shining a light through it, so it looks like the colors in your diffuse texture map were projected onto the 3D object. A planar projection is also the simplest for the computer to process, so use it if you can get the result that you need for your Android Studio application. Planar mapping is often used for static 3D objects such as billboards, because once you move (the camera) around to the sides of the 3D model, this type of projection mapping does not provide photo-real results.

Camera projection is very similar to planar projection, because a camera projects the texture from the camera lens onto a 3D object surface much like a slide projector does. The projection is 100% parallel to the front of the lens. This should be used for projecting video backgrounds onto your scene, so that you can model, or eventually animate, your 3D assets in front of the projection. If the camera moves, camera projection mapping stays parallel to the front of your lens. This is sometimes termed **billboard mapping mode** (billboard projection).

Your next simplest type is **cylindrical projection**, which provides more of a 3D application for your texture map. A cylindrical map surrounds the object in your up and down (a 3D z axis) dimension, projecting your image all the way around your object! If you walked around the 3D object, there would be unique texture details in another dimension, which planar or camera projection does not provide. Make sure that your texture maps tile seamlessly along their y axis!

An even more complex projection mapping type is called a **spherical projection**. This provided an even more complete 3D application of your texture map than the cylindrical projection does. Spherical projection attempts to address all three (x, y, and z axis) projection directions. Again, you want to make sure that your texture map is tileable to avoid any "visual seams."

Similar to a spherical projection is a **cubic projection**. It is like having six planar projections in a cube format and gives a result similar to spherical projection, using a special **cubic texture map** data format.

When you apply a cubic projection mapping type to your i3D object, the object's faces are assigned to a specific face in a **cubic texture map**, as you may have guessed. This is based on the orientation of each of the 3D object's polygon's normal, or by the proximity of the face to the cubic texture map (coordinate) UVW mapping space. The cubic texture is then projected from the faces of the cubic texture map using planar projection methods.

If you use volumetric textures, the spatial projection is a three-dimensional UVW texture projection that is projecting through the 3D object's volume. It is typically used with procedural or volumetric textures that need to have an internal structure, such as wood, marble, sponge, agate, and so forth. If you slice a 3D object, or transform texture map coordinates relative to the 3D object, different parts of the volumetric or procedural texture are subsequently revealed.

There's also a simpler texture mapping called **UV mapping** (no W dimension). This applies your textures in two dimensions instead of three, and it is easier to process because it has less data. You will probably map your 3D models outside of Android Studio by using 3D software, and then use a model importer to import your already texture mapped 3D object into Java or JavaFX. Now you're ready to take a look at the fourth dimension and 3D animation.

3D Animation: Keyframes, Motion Curves, and IK

After you have created your 3D geometry and texture mapped it using shaders and UVW mapping coordinates, you may want to make it move in some fashion; let's take a flying a helicopter model, for instance. Concepts you learned about for digital video assets apply equally as well for 3D animation assets, as you might imagine, because both use keyframes. 3D software packages have what are generally termed "track editors," which allow you to add keyframes and a "motion curve" to tracks. Each track relates to a 3D model. If a 3D model uses subcomponent grouping, then there can be tracks for groups and subgroups necessary to achieve any complex animation or simulation for your Android Studio application, game, or 3D virtual world.

Linear Animation: Tracks, Keyframes, Looping, and Ranges

The simplest type of 3D and 2D animation is **linear animation**. Linear animation uses the least amount of processing power, so it is the most efficient. If you can use linear animation to accomplish the 3D animation objective, use the fewest number of tracks and the fewest number of keyframes, as this uses the least amount of system memory. Figure 10-9 shows how to add a keyframe to the cube object in Blender 2.76 by using an "I" hotkey to access an **Insert Keyframe** menu with a cube object selected. I selected the **Delta Scale** keyframe type that adds a delta (difference) scaling value from the current scaling value.

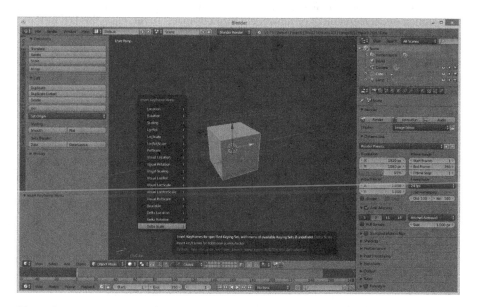

Figure 10-9. Use Insert Keyframe menu; add Delta Scale keyframe

If animation motions are repetitive, use a **seamless loop** instead of a long range containing duplicate keyframe data. One seamless motion loop can take up less memory than a long range, especially when that range contains multiple copies of the same motion, which is heavily redundant. So **looping** is a great optimization principle in linear 3D animation.

Next let's take a look at some of the more complex types of animation, including those that aren't linear. They will not be in a straight line, with evenly spaced keyframes. You'll also take a look at character animation and at procedural animation used for things like physics simulations and particle systems.

Non-Linear Animation: Motion Paths and Motion Curves

A more complex type of non-linear animation, which is less regular and often looks more realistic, especially where human motion and simple physics simulation is concerned, implements a **motion path** for the animated 3D object or element (sub-object in a hierarchy) to move along. To add even more complexity to the motion along that path, it is possible to use a **motion curve** so that the movement itself can speed up or slow down, simulating things like gravity or friction. The mathematical algorithms that are represented visually using these motion curves are called **interpolators**. JavaFX has an **Interpolator** class that contains a wide variety of the most standard (yet quite powerful, if used effectively) motion curve algorithms. You'll get into JavaFX in the next chapter, which covers 3D formats, platforms, scene graph, and programming-related topics.

A good example of non-linear irregular motion keyframing is a rubber ball bouncing down a windy road. The curved path of the road uses a motion path to make sure that the ball stays on the road curvature and that the ball floor conforms to the slope (angle) of the road. The bouncing of the ball should use a motion curve, also called a **motion interpolator**, to make each bounce look more realistic in the timing of the acceleration or deceleration of its movement through space. In this case, this is how the ball reacts to the ground.

Figure 10-10 shows a Blender Timeline editor at the bottom of the screen; it has two rotation keyframes represented as vertical yellow lines and the current frame setting is a vertical green line.

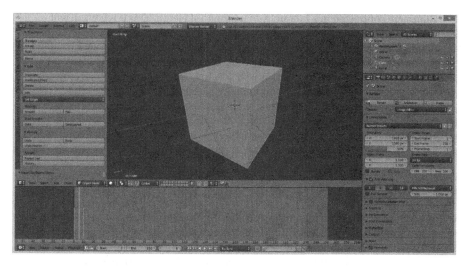

Figure 10-10. *The Blender 2.75 Timeline editor with two keyframes at Frame 0 and Frame 10 and current Frame 6 setting*

Complex physics simulation and character animation could be done using keyframes if you wanted to spend months on it; however, it is actually easier to write algorithms and code routines to achieve this than it is to lay down motion curves and keyframes to try and simulate these phenomena.

Therefore, character animation principles and procedural animation principles are covered next, as you are progressing from less advanced concepts to more advanced concepts.

Let's overview character animation next because it is the type of 3D animation that is likely to be supported in JavaFX and similar 3D platforms for Android Studio.

Character Animation: Bones, Muscles, and Inverse Kinematics

An even more complex type of animation is character animation. Character animators are one of the popular positions on a 3D film, game, or television content production team. Character animation involves a number of complex layers, including setting up bones using **inverse kinematics** to control a skeleton that attaches to the muscles and skin; so things with character animation are about as complex as they can get without using straight coding, which is called **procedural animation**. There is an animation software package that is customized for doing character animation called Hash Animation:Master, or A:M, and fortunately it has an affordable $79 annual fee to own it and to get free upgrades. It was shown in Figure 10-3. As you can see, it is an amazing product, in its 18th revision over two decades, starting as Playmation on the Amiga 3000.

At the lowest level of character animation you have your bone, which uses an inverse kinematics algorithm. This controls the range of movement (rotation), so you don't have elbows that bend the wrong way, or heads that spin around like something in *The Exorcist*.

Bones are connected in a hierarchy that forms a skeleton. This is what you will animate (keyframe) later on to bring your character to life. You can also simulate muscles and skin by attaching them to the bones, and defining how the bone movement should flex the muscles and stretch the skin for the character. The muscle flexing and skin deformations are complex algorithms as well, just like the IK algorithm that controls a range of movement for the skeleton's component parts.

As you can imagine, setting all of this up can be a very long and complex process; it is an area of character animation called "rigging." And yes, as I have mentioned for all of these areas of 3D and i3D asset creation, rigging is its very own job area if you want to work on it in the film or the console game industries. 3D is so complex that each area is its own specialty.

Procedural Animation: Physics, Fluid, Hair, and Particle Systems

The most complex type of animation is **procedural animation**, because it needs to be done using algorithms. In 3D packages, this is usually done using C++, Python, or Java. Procedural 3D animation in your Android Studio applications should be done using a combination of Java APIs, JavaFX APIs, and third-party APIs, which you will look at in the next chapter.

This is the most complex and also the most powerful type of 3D animation. It is the reason why a procedural animation programmer is another one of the more popular 3D job openings in the 3D film, games, IoT, and television production industries. You are beginning to see why i3D is the most complex new media genre, and why I saved it for the final part of the book.

There are a lot of features in 3D modeling and animation packages such as Blender, A:M, Silo, and 3D Studio Max that are actually procedural animation algorithm plugins.

The plugins expose the user interface to the user to specify parameters that control the result of a procedural animation once it is applied to 3D models or a complex 3D model hierarchy created using the 3D software.

Here are some examples of procedural animation algorithms with simulated and controlled features: particle systems, fluid dynamics, cloth dynamics, rope dynamics, hair and fur dynamics, soft body dynamics, rigid body dynamics, and video motion tracking. Many of these include real-world physics simulation support, which are often plugins added to advanced 3D animation software packages. There are many other advanced features that require algorithms to be implemented with a reasonable amount of effort. 3D is all about leveraging the computer processor and memory to create content!

Summary

In this chapter, you took a look at 3D new media concepts and terminology. You looked at 3D mesh geometry and how adding texture mapping makes this a complete 3D model. You looked at UVW mapping and how to easily apply it using projection mapping, shaders and shader language, and different types of 3D animation—from simple linear animation to complex animation types, such as character animation and procedural or algorithmic animation. You saw how complex this area of 3D new media is due to its support of advanced console games and feature film and television production.

In the next chapter, you'll learn **3D platforms and 3D file formats** using **scene graph hierarchy** 3D asset organization.

CHAPTER 11

■ ■ ■

3D New Media: Data Formats and Platforms

Now that you have an understanding of the fundamental concepts, terminology, principles, and workflow for creating 3D new media assets, it's time to take a look at how you get that 3D vector new media asset into the Android Studio environment and an Android application. Android Studio only supports one open source 3D rendering engine, called **OpenGL**, or **Open Graphics Library**, but does not yet support a **scene graph hierarchy** with which you can construct i3D or interactive 3D applications. The JavaFX API, which is actually a part of Java 7 and Java 8, but not yet included in the Android API, would solve that problem.

There are also some third-party Java platforms that now support Android and some iOS, as well as HTML5, that add scene graph capabilities to Java 7 and Android just like JavaFX does.

You will look at JavaFX and its scene graph capabilities, since JavaFX is actually a part of the Java 7, Java 8, and soon the Java 9 programming language, and also supports delivery of JavaFX applications to both the Android OS and iOS.

Then, you will look at other third-party Java scene graph platforms that you can use to create 3D or i3D applications for Android OS. You will also look at popular 3D file (data) formats that are supported in OpenGL ES 3.1 (Android), JavaFX, HTML5 WebGL, and WebGL 2. In fact, let's get that out of the way first, and then get to JavaFX scene graph and 3D platforms.

3D Model Data: Open Source File Formats

There are a number of 3D file (data) formats that used to be proprietary, such as Autodesk 3D Studio Max and Wavefront Object file formats, which are widely supported; although I am not sure if they have officially been open sourced. There are also a couple such as Collada and X3D that were intended to be open 3D data exchange formats, and a proprietary JavaFX format, which is also open source.

There is also a manufacturing 3D data file format used for injection molding machines and 3D printers, which is called the **ST**ereoLithography file format, or **STL** for short. These are outlined in Table 11-1, and most platforms import these 3D formats into their scene graph and support all of their features.

© Wallace Jackson 2015
W. Jackson, *Android Studio New Media Fundamentals*,
DOI 10.1007/978-1-4842-9867-1_11

Table 11-1. *3D Data File Formats Compatible with JavaFX in Java*

3D Format	File Extension	JavaFX 3D Model Importer	Version
Autodesk 3D Studio	.3ds	3dsModelImporterJFX	0.7
Collada	.dae or .zae	ColModelImporterJFX	0.6
JavaFX FXML	.fxml	FxmlModelImporterJFX	0.5
Wavefront Object	.obj	ObjModelImporterJFX	0.8
STereoLithography	.stl	StlModelImporterJFX	0.7
X3D Version 3.3	.x3d or .x3dz	X3dModelImporterJFX	0.4

Let's take a look at these formats and see what data can be transferred using each of them into Java 3D APIs.

Autodesk: 3D Studio for DOS 3DS

The Autodesk **3DS** format is a 3D data import and export format. It includes only the 3D mesh geometry, texture maps and light location data. The 3DS format is also supported by Autodesk 3DS Max 3D modeling, animation and rendering software, because it was the native file format of the retired Autodesk 3D Studio for DOS software, which was popular until 3D Studio MAX replaced it in 1996.

This 3DS format was designed for use with 3D Studio DOS. It was released in 1990, so it only contains basic mesh (geometry) and texture map channel data, making it a great fit for limited 3D data support currently found in OpenGL ES in Android Studio, Java (using JavaFX APIs), and HTML5 (using WebGL and WebGL 2).

The 3DS data format has become the industry standard for transferring 3D model data between 3D platforms or for offering 3D models in 3D resource data archives or 3D model storefronts.

Another popular model archiving file format is the OBJ or 3D Object file format from Wavefront. Let's look at that next.

Wavefront Technologies: Advanced Visualizer OBJ

The Wavefront Technologies Advanced Visualizer **OBJ** data format is an open source, 3D geometry definition data format. The data format has been adopted by other 3D applications and platforms.

The OBJ file format is a universally accepted basic data file format that represents 3D geometry only. Texture map data is not included in an OBJ data file, but can be referenced in a separate MTL (this stands for "materials") data file. Materials can then be referenced by data inside of the OBJ file and have to be included along with the OBJ file, which is why often 3D Objects using this format will be distributed in a ZIP file.

This OBJ data format can contain the different types of 2D and 3D data that you have learned about in Chapters 8 through 10, including vertex data, spline curves data, model hierarchy grouping data, rendering attributes data, surface (normal) attributes data, and similar advanced 3D model data structures. The most common 3D data elements are geometric vertex data, texture UVW coordinate data, face or vertex normal data, and polygon face data.

Next, let's take a look at the Collada i3D data format.

Collada: ISO Collaborative Design Activity DAE

The ISO COLLADA data format stands for **COLLA**borative **D**esign **A**ctivity. It is the i3D data interchange format for interactive 3D or i3D new media applications. It is managed by non-profit technology consortium The Khronos Group. This **DAE**, or Digital Asset Exchange, file format has been adopted by ISO as a publicly available i3D data file specification (ISO PAS 17506).

The COLLADA DAE format is the most advanced of all the 3D data formats covered in this section, as it specifically supports i3D, and therefore advanced features like physics simulations used in games, for example.

The DAE data format uses an open-standard DAE XML schema to facilitate the exchange of i3D new media assets among i3D software applications and i3D rendering platforms such as HTML5 WebGL and WebGL2, Android, and JavaFX. You learned about i3D in Chapter 10. A COLLADA data file describing i3D new media assets is actually an XML file and is identified using a .dae or .zae (a ZAE is a compressed DAE) file name extension.

Stereolithography or STL: 3D Systems CAD

The **ST**ereoLithography, or STL, data format was originally a file format that was native to the 3D Systems Stereolithography CAD software package. The STL data format is supported by other 3D software packages as well, because it is widely used for rapid prototyping, 3D printing, and computer-aided manufacturing. STL files describe only the surface geometry of 3D models, and do not include any colors, textures, or other 3D model attributes.

Because the STL file only includes polygon data, it could be looked upon as the "raw" 3D data format of these six formats you are looking at in this section of the chapter.

The data consists of triangulated surface data organized by the unit normal and the vertices for each triangle using the 3D Cartesian coordinate system. An STL vertex coordinate has to be a positive number, and there is no object scale information.

This STL data format is able to specify either an ASCII, or a binary, 3D geometry data representation. Binary files are the most common format, because it is more compact. Let's take a look at another popular ISO 3D format, the X3D data format.

X3D: The ISO Successor to VRML

The **X3D** 3D data format is an ISO standard, open source, free for commercial use, XML-defined file format for transferring 3D model and 3D scene (light and camera location) data. It is a successor to VRML, the Virtual Reality Modeling Language.

X3D includes the CAD, Geospatial, Humanoid Animation, and NURBS extensions to VRML. It has the ability to encode a scene graph hierarchy using XML syntax. It also supports VRML syntax, binary data formatting, and an enhanced application programming interface. This X3D data format supports multi-stage and multi-texture rendering, if the implementing platform allows these.

The X3D data format also supports shaders that use light mapping and normal mapping, which would be appropriate once the OpenGL ES platforms add rendering support for advanced texture map shading features (covered in Chapter 10).

FXML: The JavaFX Markup Language Data Format

Java (via JavaFX) has its own FXML 3D scene graph data format as well. This is another XML-based format and it is scriptable. It is used for constructing Java 3D object scene graphs. FXML provides an alternative to constructing scene graph hierarchies by using Java code. It is optimized for defining i3D content or defining the user interface structures for JavaFX applications.

The hierarchy structure of an FXML document needs to closely mirror, or emulate, the structure of your JavaFX scene graph. FXML is suited to constructing a pure 3D scene graph, or a 3D SubScene scene graph, or simply a 3D model consisting of JavaFX 8 Node subclasses.

You start with a **Group** class from the javafx.scene package at the top of the scene graph hierarchy, and use your javafx.scene.shape library classes—specifically **Box**, **MeshView**, **Sphere**, and **Cylinder**—to create a 3D object's geometry data.

You use the **AmbientLight** and **PointLight** classes to light your scene and the **ParallelCamera** or **PerspectiveCamera** to photograph or record video of a scene. Next, let's take a close look at the JavaFX platform, since it is built right into Java.

Java 3D Support: JavaFX Scene Graph

Because JavaFX libraries (or APIs) were integrated into Java 7, Java 8, and Java 9 to replace AWT and Swing as the "front-end" user interface design libraries for Java, I am going to cover this i3D solution first. Later on in the chapter, I will discuss other "third-party" Java solutions that work with Android, as well as iOS in some cases. Since JavaFX is now 100% integrated with Java, spanning three versions, it is just a matter of time before these libraries are added to the Android API, which upgraded from Java 6 in Android 1.x, to Java 7 in Android 5.x, and may well upgrade to Java 8 in Android 6.x, due out in 2016.

There are currently three "top-level" packages in JavaFX that contain all the support for both 2D and 3D new media asset types. The **javafx.geometry** package supports the low-level 3D geometric constructs, such as vertices, with the **Point2D** and **Point3D** classes; and areas, with the **Bounds** and the **BoundingBox** classes. A **javafx.animation** package offers low-level animation constructs such as timelines, keyframes, and motion curves, with the **Timeline**, **KeyFrame**, **KeyValue**, and **Interpolator** classes.

The **javafx.scene** package offers several nested packages, which I like to call subpackages, including **javafx.scene.shape** containing 3D shape constructs, such as the **Mesh**, **TriangleMesh**, and **MeshView** classes. A **javafx.scene.transform** package supports 2D and 3D transformations, including a **Rotate**, **Scale**, **Shear**, and **Transform** class. The **javafx.scene.paint** package contains shader classes, such as the **Material** and **PhongMaterial** classes. The **javafx.scene.media** package supports digital video with 3D geometry, using the **MediaPlayer** and **MediaView** classes.

3D Modeling: Points, Polygons, Mesh, and Shading

I split the JavaFX 3D asset support into two diagrams: one for static 3D, or rendered "still" imagery, and one for animated 3D. Interactive 3D would use all the JavaFX 3D capabilities, plus many of the Java 7, 8, and 9 API capabilities. The first diagram shows four major areas that are supported in JavaFX packages and that are important for creating **3D models**, which can be used for static 3D imagery, as well as with other JavaFX APIs, to create animated 3D content, and with Java APIs to create interactive 3D games, IoT applications, wearable apps, and 3D simulations. Figure 11-1 shows 3D models asset support.

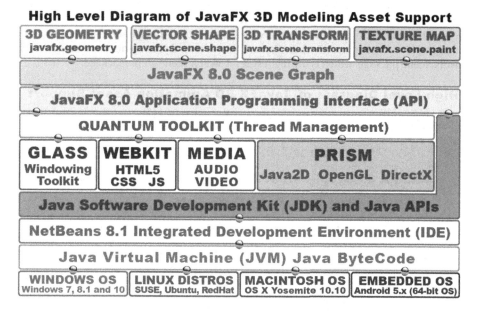

Figure 11-1. JavaFX 3D Modeling asset support showing geometry, shape, transform, and paint JavaFX APIpackages

The **javafx.geometry** package contains the foundation for all the 2D and 3D geometry in Java and JavaFX. This includes vertex (coordinated and points) and space (bounds). The **Point2D** class supports both vertex (a point in 2D space) and vector (a line in 2D space, emanating from that point) representations. A **Point3D** class also supports vertex and vector representations.

The **Bounds** superclass is used to represent your boundary of a JavaFX scene graph node, and the objects that it contains. The **BoundingBox** subclass, of the Bounds superclass, is the more specialized incarnation of a scene graph node object's boundary in 2D or 3D space, depending on the data (X,Y or X,Y,Z) used.

The **javafx.scene.shape** package contains a Mesh, MeshView, and TriangleMesh object (class). These can be used to create 3D geometry. The **javafx.scene.transform** package contains a Rotate, Scale, Shear, and Transform object (class). These can be used to apply 3D spacial transformations to your 3D mesh geometry.

121

The **javafx.scene.paint** package contains the Material and the PhongMaterial object (class). These allow you to texture 3D objects in JavaFX.

Next, let's take a look at how the JavaFX 8 API supports the fourth dimension, with 3D animation features for an Android Studio application such as a 3D game, a wearables app, or an IoT app. After that, you can look at other third-party Java 3D platforms.

3D Animation: Timeline, KeyFrame, and Interpolator

As you probably have guessed, the important classes for implementing 2D and 3D vector animation in JavaFX are stored in the **javafx.animation** package, which is seen in Figure 11-2. The exception to this is the **Camera** superclass and two subclasses named PerspectiveCamera (used in perspective camera projection) and ParallelCamera (used in orthographic camera projection). As Camera classes record your scene, these are in the **javafx.scene** package, which is the highest-level JavaFX scene graph package.

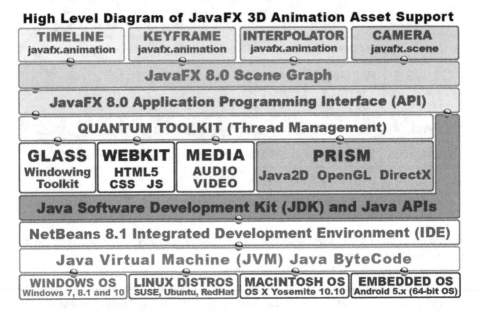

Figure 11-2. *JavaFX 3D Animation support showing animation and scene packages*

A **Timeline** object (class) holds an animation definition, which is made up of **KeyFrame** objects (class), which are in turn made up of KeyValue objects (class), which contain your actual rotation, movement, and scaling transformation instruction data.

A KeyFrame object holds an array of KeyValue objects; so a KeyFrame holds several different KeyValue data objects. There is also an **Interpolator** class, which contains a number of advanced algorithms. These apply motion curves to your KeyValue objects inside of your KeyFrame objects, inside of your Timeline object. The currently supported Interpolator algorithms include DISCRETE, EASE_IN, EASE_OUT, EASE_BOTH (easing in and out), and LINEAR straight line (even spaced) interpolation, which is the least memory and processor (processing) intensive.

Third-Party Java Scene Graph 3D Engines

There are a number of third-party engines that add scene graph and 3D capabilities to Java as well as Android Studio, and recently some of these have expanded to support iOS and HTML5. You will take a look at some of these in this section so that you have an overview of what is out there. These are all free for commercial use, and some of them provide an exceptionally professional user interface and feature set, including things like collision detection, physics simulations, 3D audio using OpenAL, 3D shaders using OpenCL, and much more.

jMonkeyEngine: The JME i3D Game Engine

The jMonkeyEngine, which you can find on jmonkeyengine.org, is a free, open source 3D Java game engine targeting Java game developers who wish to create 3D games using an i3D scene graph technology. The software is coded entirely using Java, intended to promote widespread accessibility and rapid deployment cycle. jMonkeyEngine games can be published to Windows, Mac, and Linux, as well as Android or iOS. jMonkeyEngine also supports hardware peripherals for AR and VR technologies such as the Oculus Rift. As you can see in Figure 11-3, it has impressive, professional development environment organization, which looks similar to the IntelliJ 14 Android Studio IDEA in a great many ways.

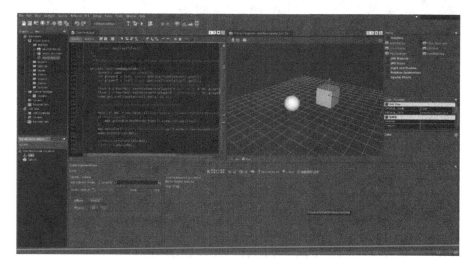

Figure 11-3. jMonkeyEngine 3.1 has a plethora of new features

jMonkeyEngine conforms to BSD licensing. jME 3.1 SDK supports its very own plugin framework, with automatic updates.

LWJGL: Lightweight Java Game Library V3

The LWJGL 3D Java library is a multiple platform implementation of popular native APIs used for the development of 3D scene graphs (OpenGL), audio (OpenAL), and parallel computing (OpenCL) applications. LWJGL provides low-level access and is not a drag-and-drop i3D development framework, so it does not provide higher-level utilities than what the native libraries expose. LWJGL is also open source software, as everything else covered in this book, and freely available for commercial use.

It is important to note that if you are a beginning Java programmer, you may want to try using one of the frameworks, or game engines, that build a user interface on top of this LWJGL3 platform before you try coding directly to the LWJGL3 library. Some of these include libGDX, which you'll look at next, as well as Slick2D, PlayN, JOGE, JMugen, GoldenT, jMonkeyEngine, Clyde, Ardor3D, Xith3D, Bonzai, Homura, JPCT, Gooei, TWL, and FengGUI.

***Figure 11-4.** Lightweight Java Game Library 3 web site lwjgl.org*

Next, let's take a look at another popular framework for 3D technology "bridging" to Java that not only makes the OpenGL framework accessible but also the **OpenAL** (3D Audio Library) and **OpenCL** (3D Computing Library) frameworks available for Java.

JOGL: Java OpenGL, OpenAL, and OpenCL

JOGL (Java OpenGL) is a wrapper library allowing OpenGL to be used in Java. It was developed by Kenneth Bradley Russell and Christopher Kline, and then further developed by Sun Microsystems.

JOGL has been an independent open source project under a BSD license since 2010. It's a **JSR-231** reference implementation for **OpenGL Java Bindings**. JOGL allows OpenGL feature access via C programming language through the use of **Java Native Interface** (JNI). JOGL allows you to access the standard OpenGL functions, as well as OpenGL Utilities. The www.jogamp.org web site shown in Figure 11-5 has more information on these **JOGL**, **JOAL**, and **JOCL** Java language bindings, as well as other interesting information.

Figure 11-5. *The jogamp.org web site, home of 3D Java libraries*

Next, you are going to look at Google Code's libGDX, which allows you to code 3D applications in Java that can span both a desktop delivery and Android delivery i3D development scenario.

libGDX: Cross-Platform Desktop and Android 3D

There is a 3D game development application framework written in Java called libGDX. It has C and C++ components for performance-optimized code as well. This allows development of desktop and mobile games with one codebase. It supports Windows, Linux, Mac OS X, Android Studio, iOS, and WebKit including WebGL or WebGL2. The libGDX uses third-party libraries LWJGL3, OpenGL, FreeType, MPG123, Vorbis, SoundTouch Audio, Box2D, OpenAL, and Kiss FFT.

Using libGDX, developers can design, code, test, and debug their application using a desktop PC, and use that same code in Android Studio. The libGDX platform assimilates the differences between Windows, Linux, and Mac desktop applications and Android Studio applications. The developer work process involves coding on your workstation while verifying that your 3D project still runs under Android. The libGDX web site is shown in Figure 11-6.

Figure 11-6. libgdx.badlogicgames.com cross-platform Java site

If you don't need a code-once-run-everywhere development scenario, and you only wish to deliver on Android OS using Android Studio, there is an **android.opengl** package that allows this as well. Let's take a look at this integrated solution next.

Android OpenGL Package: Android i3D

Android Studio includes real-time 3D rendering support with the Open Graphics Library OpenGL using an **OpenGL ES API**. OpenGL ES is the OpenGL specification intended for embedded device usage. Android supports all versions of OpenGL ES including 1.1, found in Android 1.5 to 2.2; 2.0, found in Android 2.2 to 4.3; 3.0, found in Android 4.3 to 5; and 3.1, found in Android 5 or later.

The most important Android classes that you will need to implement to leverage Android Studio to process 3D applications are the **GLSurfaceView** base class and the **GLSurfaceView.Renderer** Java interface, which makes the rendering engine refresh calls. You can find more information on these classes with at developer.android.com/reference/android/opengl/GLSurfaceView.html and developer.android.com/reference/android/opengl/GLSurfaceView.Renderer.html.

The GLSurfaceView subclass provides the base SurfaceView class implementation that provides a dedicated surface for your display of OpenGL ES rendering calls. Your GLSurfaceView object can support a number of key features, including managing the 3D surface (canvas), an area of OS memory reserved for compositing OpenGL rendered content for Android's View rendering ecosystem.

GLSurfaceView manages the EGL display enabling OpenGL to render to a surface, as well as rendering on a dedicated thread so that Android can decouple rendering performance from your UI thread. Both on-demand and continuous rendering are supported.

A GLSurfaceView object accepts a developer-provided GLSurfaceView.Renderer object, which does the actual rendering. Developers can optionally wrap, trace, or check for errors using this GLSurfaceView.Renderer object's OpenGL calls.

As a default, the GLSurfaceView object creates a surface using the **PixelFormat.RGB_888** format surface. If you require an alpha—that is, a translucent surface, then you use the `.getHolder().setFormat(PixelFormat.TRANSLUCENT)` method call structure instead, so that you get the **PixelFormat.ARGB_8888** format.

Implement GLSurfaceView by subclassing it and overriding one of the View system input event methods. If your application doesn't require event processing, GLSurfaceView may be used as-is. A GLSurfaceView object can be customized by calling `.set()` methods (instead of subclassing). Unlike a normal View, drawing is delegated to a separate GLSurfaceView.Renderer object, which is registered with GLSurfaceView by using a `.setRenderer(`**Renderer**`)` call. To initialize GLSurfaceView, call `.setRenderer(Renderer)`.

Summary

In this chapter, you took a look at popular open i3D file formats as well as some i3D platforms for Java, such as JavaFX, jMonkeyEngine, LWJGL3, libGDX, and the android. opengl package, all of which can be used in conjunction with Android Studio.

In the next chapter, you will take a look at how the new media assets that you've been learning in book are referenced inside of Android Studio 1.4, which as you know, develops applications for the Android 5.4 OS.

CHAPTER 12

■ ■ ■

Referencing New Media Assets in Android Studio

Now that we have covered new media content for Android Studio, it's time to take a look at how these new media assets, which you will create using all your newfound multimedia production knowledge, are integrated in Android Studio. The foundation for this knowledge is where these assets need to be in your Android Studio project, in order to be referenced correctly in the Java code or in the XML markup, if you prefer to set things up that way.

This chapter covers the different Drawable-DPI folders for image assets and the raw folder for video or audio assets. You will also learn how a 2D or 3D vector asset should be referenced in Android Studio. And you'll look at how new media assets are referenced in app user interface design and for straight content display.

Android Assets: Drawables and Raw Data

As you learned in Chapter 2, pixel-based digital imagery is technically called raster imagery, because an array of pixel values is rasterized to a screen displaying the image created using these pixels. Digital illustration, or vector imagery, is not stored as an array of image elements (pixels), it's instead drawn, or "rendered," to the screen, just like you would draw it if someone were watching you draw, only using instructions that the computer uses to do exactly what you did when you created it.

This is the equivalent of the MIDI concept that you learned about in Chapter 4, which focused on digital audio, where the performance is re-created by the computer processor, which renders it to the screen (SVG) or the synthesizer (MIDI) using playback instructions.

Android Resources: Assets Subfolder Hierarchy

If you want to add custom animation, custom themes, digital video, digital audio, or vector assets to your Android project, you might have to add new folders to your project folder hierarchy; you will learn how to do this in this chapter. In this section, I want to give you an overview of different project resource folder names, and the new media asset types that are possible in an Android Studio application. This gives you a high-level overview of what's possible in Android development.

© Wallace Jackson 2015
W. Jackson, *Android Studio New Media Fundamentals*,
DOI 10.1007/978-1-4842-9867-1_12

Your external new media assets—that is, those primarily created outside of Android, using software such as GIMP 2.8 and Audacity 2.1—are kept in the resources folder. In Figure 12-1, this folder is open to show various resource subfolders for the 2D project that I created for my *Pro Android Wearables* (Apress, 2015) book. These are only half of the potential folder names.

Figure 12-1. *Resource subfolders for ProAndroidWearable project*

Other non-multimedia resource assets can also be kept in the project resource directory's subfolders, including styles, constants, themes, colors, animation, application icon mipmaps, XML definition files, and user interface layout definitions.

Externalizing resources allows an Android Studio project development work process to be more modular and organized, and therefore more quickly accessed during apps development. There are many different resource types in Android and they either have their own **subfolders** in a /res project folder, or their own **XML files** in a /res/values folder. I'll outline the ten primary resource subfolder names and the asset types that they hold in Table 12-1. Because they are very important to Android development, I'll discuss the ones that relate to the new media assets you have learned in this book. The ones that relate to new media are **anim**, **drawable**, **mipmap**, and **raw**.

Table 12-1. *Android Studio Project Resource Subfolder Types*

Resource Subfolder	Types of Assets That the Resource Subfolder Contains
Animator	XML definitions containing property animation
Anim	XML definitions containing 2D frame animation
Color	XML definitions containing color constants
Drawable	Digital image assets (PNG8, PNG24, PNG32)
Mipmap	Digital image application icons (PNG32)
Layout	XML definitions for user interface layouts
Menu	XML definitions containing menu structures
Raw	Digital video, digital audio, SVG, 3D formats
Values	XML definitions containing property values
Xml	XML definitions containing non-Android XML

The primary types of new media resources include digital image assets that go in the /res/drawable folder; digital video and digital audio resources that go in the /res/raw folder; digital image or digital video procedural animation, or movement, rotation, and scaling, which go in the /res/anim folder; and finally, the Android application icon PNG32 digital image assets, which go into the /res/mipmap folder.

The names defined in Table 12-1 are standardized Android Studio folder names; that is, they're "hard-coded" into the OS and have code that specifically looks for them in this /res folder. You can define your own customized folder names as long as you follow basic **folder naming rules**. These folders are termed "alternate" folders, because they provide **alternative assets**.

Alternate Resource Folders: Custom Folder Names

You can also provide something called **alternate resource folders** in your Android application project folder hierarchy. The alternate resource folders provide custom asset support for a wide array of device physical hardware specifications by grouping new media assets, user interface designs, styles, and theme definitions into specifically named alternate resource folders. A good example of this is the /res/drawable-dpi folder hierarchy, which the Eclipse IDE created for you prior to Android 5. Android used to create a /res/drawable-hdpi folder and a /res/drawable-xhdpi folder for different pixel density image assets to be stored in. Different density drawable image assets are covered in the next section of this chapter.

Alternate resource folders allow developers to design an app so that it works across a range of consumer electronics hardware devices, from smartwatches to UHD iTV sets. For digital images, this equates to providing more than one version for each asset, using different pixel densities, or lower to higher resolution assets to fit widely different screen hardware resolutions.

For user interface designs, this equates to providing more than one design. Different UI layouts use different aspect ratios, specifically portrait, known as **port** in Android, and landscape, known as **land** in Android. UI layouts take screen resolution into account as well, using a width (w#dp), height (h#dp) and a smallest width (sw#dp) folder naming convention. There's also a widescreen folder naming convention called **long**, and a normal screen naming convention, called **notlong**. Screen sizes are also grouped into four basic naming convention categories: **small**, **normal** (medium), **large**, and **xlarge** (extra-large). Table 12-2 shows these folder naming conventions, all in one location.

Table 12-2. *Android OS Alternate Folder Naming Conventions*

Name Modifier	Purpose for Using This Alternate Folder Name Modifier
Land	Screen uses a landscape or sideways orientation
Port	Screen uses a portrait or up-and-down orientation
Long	Screen uses a widescreen aspect ratio
notlong	Screen uses a normal screen aspect ratio (not wide)
sw#dp	Smallest screen width required by name modifier
w#dp	Width of screen required by folder name modifier
h#dp	Height of screen required by folder name modifier
small	Small display screen (smartwatch, flip phone)
normal	Medium display screen (smartphone, mini tablet)
large	Large display screen (tablet, netbook, laptop)
xlarge	Extra-large display screen (HD or UHD iTV set)

At runtime—that is, when your application is being run—Android OS uses your appropriate alternate resource folder assets based on the device screen hardware specifications.

For example, if you want to provide different UI design layouts that conform to physical screen sizes, shapes, or orientations (portrait and landscape), you can define a user interface layout design using custom UI layout folder names.

For instance, you could define a /res/layout-land folder for a landscape-specific UI layout design or a /res/layout-port for a portrait-specific UI layout design. If you wanted to make sure that you have at least 720 pixels of screen width for your portrait UI design, you would create a /res/layout-port-sw720dp folder. For a UI design for HDTV or UHDTV, you could specify a/res/layout-land-sw1920dp folder that targets HD or UHD iTV set widescreen resolutions. To target only UHD devices, you could use /res/layout-land-sw3840dp, /res/layout-port-sw4096dp, or /res/layout-port-sw2160dp for UHD smartphones.

Next, let's take a look at Android Drawable objects and screen density modifiers, because these also directly relate to what you have learned in this book.

Android Drawable: Draw Assets to Any DPI Screen

A **drawable** in Android is any graphic that can be drawn on your display. I've listed device DPI density constants in Table 12-3.

Table 12-3. *Seven Android Studio Device Density DPI Constants*

Device DPI	Screen Size Constant	Pixel Density in DPI	Pixel Multiply Index	Minimum Screen Dimension	Launch Icon Size	Action Bar Icon	Notify Icon Size
LDPI Low Density	small	120	0.75	426×320	36×36	24×24	18×18
MDPI Medium	normal	160	1.0	470×320	48×48	32×32	24×24
TVDPI HD 1280	HDTV	213	1.33	1280×720	64×64	48×48	32×32
HDPI High Density	large	240	1.5	640×480	72×72	48×48	36×36
XHDPI Extra High	xlarge	320	2.0	960×720	96×96	64×64	48×48
XXHDPI Super High	xxlarge	480	3.0	1280×960	144×144	96×96	72×72
XXXHDPI Ultra High	xxxlarge	640	4.0	1920×1080	192×192	128×128	96×96

Drawables—that is, your digital image and digital video assets—need to be categorized for your Android apps according to the seven screen density constants listed in Table 12-3.

If you look at the three columns on the right side of Table 12-3, you see that you need to create UI elements such as application launch, notification, and action bar icons for each of these screen density levels to support all the thousands of hardware devices in the market that use the Android OS. If you need more advanced digital imaging than what is covered in Chapters 2 and 3, there is a *Digital Image Compositing Fundamentals* (Apress, 2015) book that might help take your digital image editing and compositing knowledge up a level or two. This work process is also discussed in my *Android Apps for Absolute Beginners Third Edition* title (Apress, 2013).

There are several types of drawable assets that need to be placed (located, kept, or stored) in the drawable folder for these assets to be visible to and accessible to an Android application. The primary one is BitmapDrawable, which I cover in the next section, as well as media assets that are created with bitmaps, such as **frame animation**.

Any assets that reference bitmaps or frame animation in an XML definition file format are also kept in this folder, as would any XML definitions creating ShapeDrawables (2D vector illustration). Vector shapes are covered in detail in my *Digital Illustration Fundamentals* (Apress, 2015) book.

Drawable Objects: Referencing Assets in Memory

There are many different types of drawable objects in Android, each of which has its own class to allow you to fine-tune the attributes of that drawable and to reference it in system memory as a Java object so that you can use it in an app.

Some of the important Drawable types are **BitmapDrawable**, which references your digital image asset **ShapeDrawable**, which references your digital illustration assets; **NinePatchDrawable**, which references tileable PNG 9-patch assets; **AnimationDrawable**, which references your animation assets; **LayerDrawable**, which is used to composite image assets into layers; **TransitionDrawable**, which is used to transition or fade your image assets into each other; **ScaleDrawable**, which can be used to resample (scale) any image assets; **ClipDrawable**, which can be used to clip (crop) an image asset; **InsetDrawable**, which is used to place an image asset inside of another drawable; **StateListDrawable**, which defines image assets for different states; and **LevelListDrawable**, which defines an image asset for each level, such as signal levels on your smartphone signal level indicator, for instance. You will want to research each Drawable class, before using it!

If you want to dive into these graphics classes at the professional Android level, check out *Pro Android Graphics* (Apress 2013), which covers all of these Drawable objects, classes, and assets, as well as the workflow necessary to implement them inside of your Android Studio applications. Next, let's take a look at how new media assets can be utilized for Android user interface design.

Android Layout: Assets Used in XML UI Designs

The layout in Android is aptly named, as it is a definition of how your user interface elements and Drawable assets are going to be "laid out" relative to each other on your Android device display screen. Chances are that if you want an Android app to have a custom design for each genre of device (iTV set, smartphone, tablet, smartwatch), you are going to have a number of these custom /res/layout folders, not just a /res/layout-land and a /res/layout-port folder, as I used as examples earlier.

You'll probably also have a large number of complex alternate resource folders, such as /res/layout-sw800dp-land for tablets, /res/layout-sw1280dp-port-long for smartphones, and /res/layout-sw240dp-land for smartwatches. The more of them you define, the more perfectly the app will morph between different manufacturers' Android hardware device products.

Your /res/layout folder and any custom layout alternate resource folders that you may create generally contain UI layout XML definition files.

These are user interface designs, which are handcrafted using XML markup and stored in *filenamehere*.xml files. These files are located in the /res/layout folder or one of the alternate layout resource folders that you have created.

Since this is your *Android Studio New Media Fundamentals* book and not an Android programming book, I will leave both XML and Java programming to other more specialized books, such as my *Pro Android UI* (Apress, 2014) title, for instance.

Asset Referencing: The Android Resources Class

Android OS has an application resource system that keeps track of all non-programming assets associated with your application. You can use an Android **Resource** class to access the application resources. This Resource class is a **public** class, which extends the **java.lang.Object** base class, meaning it was scratch-coded by the Android OS development team specifically to provide resources for your Android Studio project. The Java class hierarchy for the Resources class therefore looks like the following:

```
java.lang.Object
  > android.content.res.Resources
```

The Resources class has one known direct subclass named **MockResources**. Another unrelated class, **ResourceCompat**, can also be used to access resources across all previous versions of the Android OS. Generally, however, you want to use the Resources class. You should acquire the Resources instance associated with your application with **getResources()**. So to import one of your digital image assets, you would use a .getResources.getDrawable (int id, Resources.Theme theme) method call.

It is important to note that the simpler version of this method call, .getResources. getDrawable (int id) was deprecated in Android API Level 22. This was probably to force developers to explicitly declare the Theme object when getting a drawable.

So in your existing Android Java code, if you have a Java statement that looks like this:

getResources().getDrawable(**R.drawable.**your_drawable_name_here)

You should replace it with the following Java statement:

Resources.getDrawable(**getResources()**, R.drawable.your_drawable_name, **null**)

The null means "use the current Theme object defined for my application." The R, as you know as an Android developer, equates to the /res folder, and the .drawable to your /drawable subfolder. These are symbols that are used to reference a new media asset. So the layout definition is in R.layout.name, which references an XML UI layout definition file. Again, this is all information that you should already know. I am just including it here for the sake of completeness.

Therefore, **R.drawable.filename** in Android Studio Java is the equivalent of the path structure /res/drawable/filename.png, but then again, as an Android developer, you already know that.

Android's SDK tool compiles an application resources hierarchy into your application binary at build time. To use a new media asset as a resource, you must install it correctly in your project /res directory folder hierarchy, and then build an application once all the assets are installed in the correct folder names, as I outlined in this chapter.

As part of the application's Gradle build process, the SDK tool generates symbols for each resource, which you can use in your application code to then directly access the resources.

Using application resources such as external new media assets, UI layout definitions, and constants make it easy to update various characteristics of your application without having to modify your Java code, which is really convenient as your application size and complexity increases.

More importantly, by providing a significant number of alternative resources using the alternate resource subfolder naming conventions, you are able to optimize an application for a wide variety of Android hardware device genres and different manufacturer device configurations.

You can also leverage this capability to fine-tune and customize an application for different languages, screen sizes, aspect ratios, and pixel densities, all based upon the constant tables saliently outlined in this chapter.

Along with using the new media asset knowledge from this book to its maximum capability, using the resources "tricks and tips" in this last chapter should be a very important aspect of developing your Android application. If you make an application that is widely compatible across different types of devices, it equates to significantly more sales, which improves the profits for your bottom line.

Summary

In this final chapter, you took a look at some of the key issues in Android Studio regarding referencing new media assets inside of the Android SDK and OS. You looked at supported folder naming constants, seven pixel density constants, almost a dozen different types of Drawable objects, how to correctly create alternate resource folder names, and how to use the Resources or ResourcesCompat classes to import your new media assets into the system memory for use inside of your multimedia-savvy Android Studio applications.

Of course, this has only been a review for all of you Android developers, but I wanted to include it here to be thorough and to show you how all the new media asset types covered over the course of this book hook into Android Studio projects and the Android SDK and OS.

I hope you have enjoyed this exploration of what Android can do with new media assets, and that you'll explore using new media in your Android Studio applications in the near future.

Index

© Wallace Jackson 2015
W. Jackson, *Android Studio New Media Fundamentals*,
DOI 10.1007/978-1-4842-9867-1

▓ U

▓ V

Printed in the United States
By Bookmasters